DRESSING RICH

by Leah Feldon

DRESSING RICH
WOMANSTYLE

DRESSING RICH

A Guide to Classic Chic
for Women with
More Taste than Money

by LEAH FELDON

Illustrated by June Reynard

A PERIGEE BOOK

Perigee Books
are published by
The Putnam Publishing Group
200 Madison Avenue
New York, New York 10016

LIBRARY OF CONGRESS CATALOGING IN PUBLICATION DATA

Feldon, Leah, date.
Dressing rich.

1. Clothing and dress. 2. Fashion. I. Title.
TT507.F435   1984   646'.34   83-23739
ISBN 0-399-50980-1

First Perigee printing, 1984
PRINTED IN THE UNITED STATES OF AMERICA
Designed by Helen Barrow
1 2 3 4 5 6 7 8 9

For my mother—who has always managed
to look like a million
on considerably less.

Acknowledgments

Special thanks to those whose energies are part of this book: My family and friends for their constant support and inspirations; Paul and Henrietta Kahan, Eda Baruch, Betsy Cameron, David O'Grady, Margaretta Stupakoff, Peter Morrison. And Ray Garcia and Shelley Smith—not only for their support but for contributing their time and talents to the cover photo. And to those whose insights were indeed a help: Joan Sibley, Amy Greene, Helen Murray, Stanley Weaver, M. Marc, Joan Davidson, Susan Galbraith, and Diane Smith. And to my editor, Diane Reverand, and her assistant, Melissa Pierson, for their invaluable assistance and patience. My agent, Connie Clausen, for all her positive input. And to artist June Reynard for her wonderful illustrations, dedication, and eighteen-hour days.

Contents

Introduction

You don't need a lot of money to Dress Rich. It's easy to look elegant, opulent, and chic and still remain happily solvent. Dressing Rich is a simple matter of mind over money. *As you will learn in these pages, what you lack in capital you can make up for with solid know-how, resourcefulness, and a good, viable strategy. All of these, I might add, are ultimately a better guarantee of good dressing than a substantial bank account—and, fortunately, much more easily acquired.*

Dressing Rich is essentially dressing with elegance and taste. It is the understated, sophisticated, classic, status look that has been the unmistakable signature of stylish women from Garbo to Jackie O. and undoubtedly will continue to be a mark of class regardless of prevailing fads and trends. Dress styles will, of course, change from year to year, but the basic concept of elegance and classic chic defies time and will remain a winning constant.

Dressing well takes a little practice, just like anything you want to excel in. But more than practice, it takes a real awareness. Chances are you already know more than you think. During my many years in the fashion business, clients and friends have come to me for advice and help in putting together their wardrobes. The conversations usually begin with comments like, "I have absolutely no fashion sense. . . . I have no idea what looks good on me. I'm not even sure what I like anymore. Help!" When we do meet it always turns out that they are much better informed than they think they are. They just haven't allowed themselves to tune their knowledge in. They recognize easily enough when someone else is well dressed and can almost always point out the quality specifics. They can look through fashion magazines and quickly distinguish the tasteful from the tacky. But when it comes to themselves they seem to lose all objectivity. Their innate fashion sense goes down the drain, they clench up, decisions become agonizing. Instead of letting themselves go and trusting their instincts, they start to worry, "Is this in fashion?" "Will Bob like this?" "Will this create the right impression?" and so on till they totally intimidate themselves and fashion becomes a complete enigma.

Most of these concerns are assuredly valid. You do want to make a good impression. You want to look up-to-date, and, of course, you want to be well dressed. What you do not want to do is overthink yourself into a state of paralysis. Fashion should be fun—not a burden.

I've always considered fashion a pleasure, but I'm sure part of the reason is that I've had a very objective view of it. It has been my job as a New York fashion stylist for more than twelve years to select clothes and accessories for ads and television commercials. Putting together smashing outfits, choosing the right accessories, understanding and working with the subtleties of proportion, and shopping were just part of the job. So I felt none of the personal anxieties that many women feel when getting together their own wardrobes. Dressing others is always easier than dressing yourself. I was lucky to have such nonsubjective training.

In my last book, Womanstyle, I tried to share some of this objectivity, take some of the mystery out of fashion, and show how fun it all can be. Here I'm going to get more specific. We will concentrate on the fashion principles that are the foundation of elegant dressing— dressing well—and dressing rich. In these pages I will give you the solid guidelines and background information you will need to relax, to enjoy the "New Elegance" in fashion, and to dress with ultimate taste and self-assurance.

The major advantages to following my Dressing Rich system are explicit. First is the confidence it allows. Classic chic will take you gracefully through every situation with style and class, and it is always a very comforting and secure feeling to know you can go anywhere and never feel out of place. Nothing can put more of a damper on a social or work situation than feeling overdressed, underdressed, or just plain badly dressed. We've all been in this distressing predicament at one time or another, and I'm sure we all agree that the experience hardly warrants a repeat performance. With this plan, you can be sure there'll be no encore.

Benefit number two is the positive image you will project. There is no question that we are initially judged by our outward appearance and dealt with accordingly. To put it in black-and-white terms, look like a panhandler and you'll be treated like one. But look like a countess and you'll be treated like a countess. It's as simple as that, and who wouldn't agree that the royal treatment wins, hands down? The point is that our clothing is as much a part of the first impression we make as our demeanor is, and we might as well take advantage of that fact. If we ignore it, it won't just go away. A classically chic look opens doors that might otherwise be closed—in all facets of life. To be comfortable in society's more elite circles, to better your career standing, or simply to improve your lot in life, you have to dress the part. No image is better suited to these purposes than classic chic.

* * *

If there were ever a perfect time to rediscover and reap the rewards of traditional elegance it is now, when the fashion industry is 100 percent behind you. The "look of class" is officially in. The New York Times Magazine *has referred to it as "Opulent Dressing" and even happily reports that "the elegant look is au courant for children too."* Women's Wear Daily *has delicately dubbed it "snob dressing." Others herald it as "a classic renaissance." No matter what you call it, it's clear that the time has come to put your plastic high heels and rhinestone-studded T-shirts out to pasture, at least for the remainder of this decade.*

Reagan's Washington certainly serves as an excellent sign of the times. Aside from the President's casual but classy riding habit and the First Lady's overall chic, the level of elegance at the White House has been upgraded across the board: tacky old reliable Styrofoam coffee cups have been replaced by spanking new china vessels. Blue jeans have been banished, women's slacks discouraged, and a jacket and tie are de rigueur *for men.*

The revival of traditional elegance is really not surprising when you stop to consider the current mood of the country. Fashion is always a reflection of the times, and America is, without question, presently on a very conservative course. The current state of the nation is rather timely and fortunate for the fashion industry, which, on the whole, was bewildered and generally unprepared to cope with the unconventional dress habits and cavalier attitudes of the "Woodstock Generation." The jeans revolution and its no-rules dress code left the industry in shock, with designers, buyers, and consumers alike scurrying every which way in the search for a unified look. Well, at last, Seventh Avenue can lean back and take a deep breath. We now have, if not a totally unified look, at least a solid fashion direction that will take us through most of the decade with ease and classic good taste.

I'm the last one to hop on the fashion bandwagon to advocate a particular look simply because it's what's happening at the moment, as you already know if you have read Womanstyle. *I have always been a rebellious sort, opposed to blindly following fashion's whims and trends. In this rare case, however, the current trends are in perfect harmony with my basic fashion philosophy, which is individualistic and at the same time traditional. Dressing Rich is, by happy circumstance, timely, but it incorporates all of my fashion beliefs and theories that will never be outdated: investment buying, quality recognition, a compact and select wardrobe, practicality, style, and— most importantly—elegance.*

In many ways, elegance is like beauty. It is skin deep. Certainly fashion is a big factor. But I must note that fashion is only part of our total presentation. The rest comes from within: our attitudes, spirit, quality of voice, carriage, and humor. It is, after all, the woman who makes the clothes, not the clothes the woman. To see this clearly you only have to consider how easily a shrill voice and a bag-swinging, streetwalker stride could make mincemeat of even the most exquisitely chic ensemble.

Ultimately, Dressing Rich is classic elegance. It is a fine, harmonious blend of personal style and good taste, fashion savvy and awareness, attitude and grooming, and a recognition and appreciation of quality. Elegance is the universally accepted and admired look of the true rich—those rich in style and taste, not necessarily in stock portfolios and private islands.

1

THE PHILOSOPHY: THE ESSENCE OF ELEGANCE

Classic Fashion Concepts

BEFORE WE TAKE a deep look into the classic fashion concepts and plot our course to elegance, I feel it's worthwhile to review some of the other popular American status looks. Not that any of them, of course, can hold a candle to classic chic, but they are, in their own way, legitimate and prosperous looks. The two main drawbacks of these contenders is that, to create them, each requires a lot of hard cash or at least blue bloodlines in the family. And none is ultimately universal—that is to say none fares terribly well outside its immediate environment.

Why then even give these styles an honorable mention? Well, even though they pale in comparison to classic chic, these looks of comfort have positive and negative aspects that we can learn from.

Although these affluent styles seem to have developed, and are still flourishing, regionally, they are no longer strictly indigenous to their native areas. It is, after all, a small world that we live in. You might recognize these styles from their names alone, but after this brief listing we will analyze them one at a time to see what wisdom they have to offer us.

- East Coast Old Guard
- Lone Star Chic (including not only Texas but "the rest of the West")
- L.A. Throwaway and Hollywood Flash
- Southern California Republican, or Mainstream Panache
- Palm Beach Pizzazz
- All-American Prepette

East Coast Old Guard

"OLD GUARD," OF COURSE, means very old money. How old is not necessarily important, although it does seem to have a direct effect on the degree of dowdiness—the older the money, the greater the "dowd." Since members of the Old Guard go out of their way not to display their wealth, their clothes and accessories may not look expensive at first glance. Only after careful scrutiny will you realize that their clothing is A-number-one choice quality. And since the Old Guard are notoriously tight with a buck, the clothes may not be new, but then, even the oldest cardigan was a gem in its day. Quality fabrics and superior workmanship—if not always the greatest styling—are a signature of the ECOG.

Practicality and comfort take absolute priority over the whims of fashion (which is probably why even the youngest of the Old Guard look like the old Old Guard). Trends and fads are not even in the vocabulary of the ECOG, and there is a conspicuous lack of interest in what's in vogue. "If it was good enough for grandmother it is certainly good enough for me," appears to be the overriding fashion philosophy, in makeup and hair styles as well as clothing.

A typical Old Guard look can run the gamut from Eleanor Roosevelt to Rose Kennedy; Mrs. Kennedy, of course, being on the most contemporary and snappy side of the Old Guard fashion spectrum. Whether it's a long, dark, wool skirt worn with a seasoned cashmere turtleneck and a string of pearls for a casual fall evening at home, or a cool, light-blue piqué costume and pearls for a few hours of chauffeured shopping, Old Guard fashion is never frivolous and always very sensible.

These women, with their very proper posture and unmistakable air of confidence, bolstered by generations of wealth and power, exude a kind of royal authority that counteracts any possible fashion fault—and they always look rich.

The lessons to be learned:

1. Quality pays off.

2. Trends and fads should not be arbitrarily accepted.

3. Comfort and practicality count.

4. Attitude is one-half the battle.

5. A complete lack of interest in voguish styles works against you. It's important to keep abreast of fashion to make slight wardrobe and style adjustment.

Lone Star Chic

LONE STAR CHIC takes a tack opposite to that of the Old Guard. Its philosophy: If you've got it, flaunt it. No holds are barred. There is no humility here about scads of money. After all, it took a lot of true grit, cows, and oil wells to make it, and, by gosh, they're going to enjoy it. Therefore, all jewelry is out of the vaults and, like everything else in Texas, it is *big*. Furs are often sighted on lukewarm

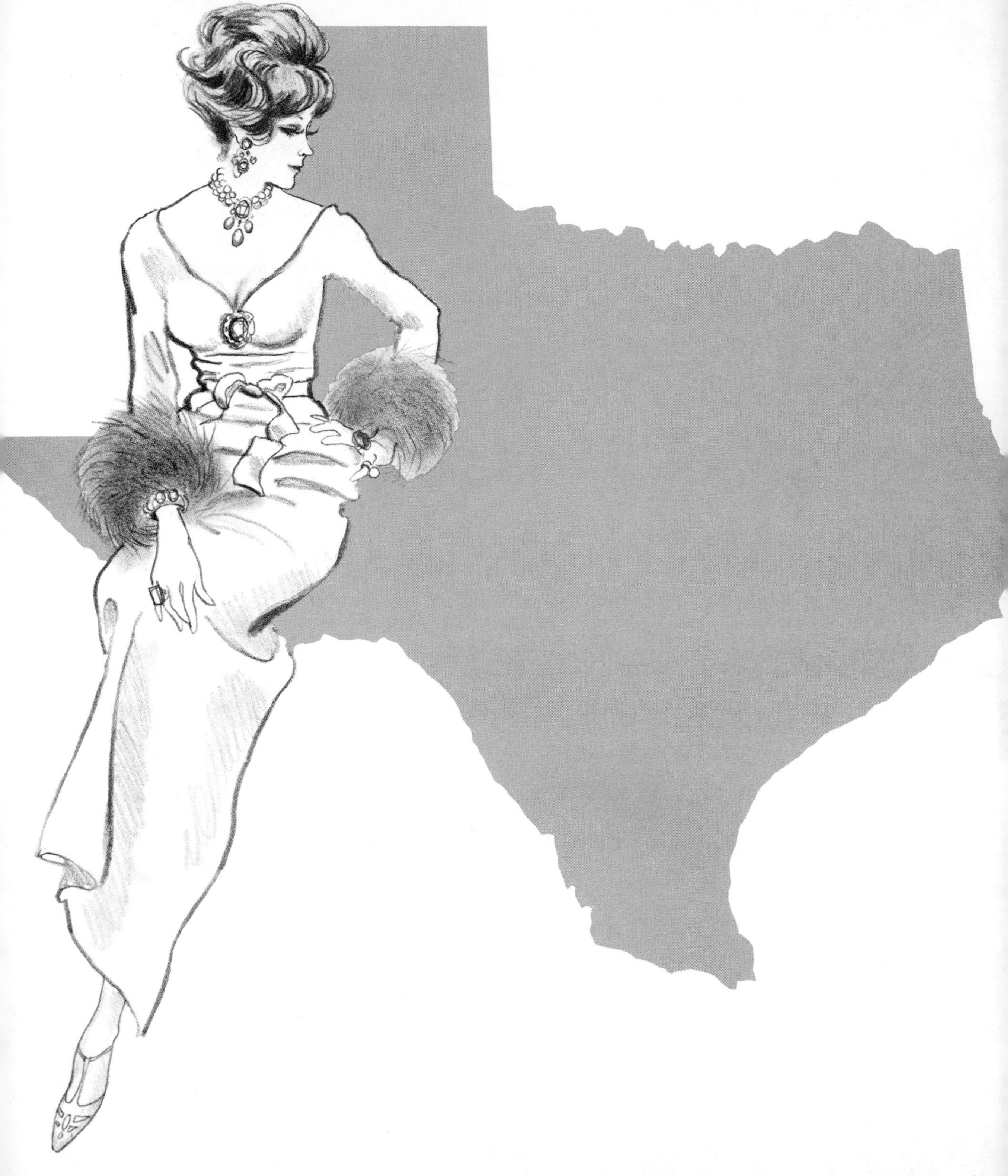

evenings. Subtlety is obviously not the issue here.

Although quality counts, being *au courant* has at least an equal footing. LSC women do their darnedest to keep up with the times, even if the current trends are not particularly flattering. Costly garments are commonly discarded after only a few major appearances. Tight-fitting, body-sculpting fashions are often preferred to the looser, more comfortable variety. Color range is as vast as the open plains.

Curiously, although interest in fashion is prime, the Lone Star group seem to hold on to outmoded makeup and hair styles as long as possible. Teased hair and false eyelashes are the living testimonials. It is the down-home friendliness and open attitude toward life that make these women charming, rather than their sense of fashion.

The lessons here:

1. It's not a good idea to wear all your jewelry at one time (especially considering the current crime rates in most cities).

2. Outdated hair and makeup will make even the best of fashions look unchic.

3. Interest in fashion is a good thing, but attention must also be paid to individual style.

4. Fit is everything, and tight is not all right.

5. Wait for the cold weather to bring out the furs.

6. A warm, friendly attitude is always a plus.

L.A. Throwaway and Hollywood Flash

THESE LOOKS were born of the film industry and are now part and parcel of the music and television industries as well.

LATs have lots of money, usually from their $500,000 salaries (plus bonuses), million-dollar contracts, or two-million-dollar deals. They are young, or they look young (thanks to the best cosmetic surgery money can buy), and are very health and body conscious. Their fashions confirm their wealth: diamond stud earrings, gold Rolex watch, Louis Vuitton bag, Yves Saint Laurent jacket and blouse . . . but there is always something that is a throwaway—three-year-old Levi's (worn with the Saint Laurents), or maybe cowboy boots—always something there that lets you know that even though they are obviously swimming in money they are still "real folk." Of course, the Rolls-Royce helps the confirmation, too.

With the vogue running so strongly in a more elegant and formal direction, LATs will no doubt be dressing a bit more conservatively too. But they will never be out-and-out establishment dressers. They may know and appreciate the fine things in life, but they are still flower children at heart.

While you might think that aspiring starlets fall into the L.A. Throwaway category as well, they are really in a class by themselves: Hollywood Flash. Unless a Hollywood starlet is under the wing of a "generous" movie mogul, she cannot yet afford the necessary L.A. status accoutrements to pull off a legitimate throwaway look. So, rather than downplaying what she doesn't have, she completely overdoes it and pretends to have

L.A. Throwaway

Hollywood Flash

more than she actually does. She can most often be seen in wonderful borrowed gowns and shocking, glittery ensembles that fully display all her wares and accomplish the all-important goal of standing out in a crowd. And she does.

Once a starlet is discovered and has a few million of her own she can afford to put on the old Levi's—and then pull the new Rolls deftly out from the three-car garage.

Lessons:

1. Sometimes it's fun to break the rules.
2. Quality is important.
3. It's great to be rich, and, when that's the case, you don't always have to take fashion too seriously.
4. If you've got it, by all means enjoy it.

Palm Beach Pizzazz

CONTRARY TO THE NAME, PBPs are not all that pizzazzy. Palm Beach Pizzazz is the only real contribution from the southern territory. The rest of the South is an amalgamation of our other looks. PBP is actually the spiritual and tropical counterpart of the Old Guard. The tweeds of the north have been appropriately translated into cool linens, fine cottons, silks, and, yes, even a hint of polyester (practicality ever present). Wool still has a slight stronghold in the form of the white blazer and is most commonly seen with navy skirt or trousers. Aside from the navy, colors have gone tropical and often match the swaying palm trees and pink-stucco mansions. Golf clothes are *de rigueur* and long evening gowns still grace the ballrooms. Palm Beach is the only place on the continent with more Rolls-Royces per capita than Los Angeles. And they make as fine an accessory here as anywhere.

To learn:

1. A tropical climate does not preclude a rich look.

2. Lifestyle is important in establishing your wardrobe.

3. Money doesn't mean universal chic.

4. Navy and white *is* a rich combination.

Southern California Republican, or Mainstream Panache

THIS IS THE other main offering from the West Coast, but it now has a stronghold on the upper middle class in most parts of the nation. At its best, SCR can be quite tasteful and dignified. At its worst it can be boring, but it is never inelegant. Nancy Reagan is a prime example of SCR at its best (while Pat Nixon perhaps exemplifies it at its worst).

These women could not be said to have great individual flair, but they do have a good amount of fashion savvy and the excellent sense to choose top designers with whom they have affinity (rather than because he might have the latest image) and stick with them for long intervals. They are always impeccably groomed with never a hair out of place.

If there's any real fault with the look it is the lack of a genuinely personal touch that is indicative of true style. Yet this is not a harsh pronouncement, since true style is such a rare thing. All in all, SCR women do rather well in creating an aura of elegance.

Lessons:

1. Grooming is extremely important and is indispensable to creating a rich look.

2. If you can afford the counseling and designs of the top designers—go for them.

3. There's something to be said for conservatism.

All-American Prepette

LAST BUT HARDLY LEAST we have the All-American Prepette. This is the most popular and widely acclaimed of all the American status looks. It has received so much attention and media coverage that by now most of you can spot a Prepette a mile away. For those of you who have somehow managed to miss all the mentions of prep dress, like *The Official Preppy Handbook*, I'll give you a quick rundown of fundamental prep fashion.

Of all the mini-status looks, the Prepette is the most blatantly American and comes the closest of all to being an actual uniform. The prep look (and actually some of the clothes) can take a woman comfortably and directly from her finishing school days right through to her country club years (after forty). The look is solid, and there is little outside fashion influence.

Although ultimately practical and understated, Prepettes could hardly be termed chic. One of the more notable earmarks of the Prepette is her penchant for primary colors and brilliant pastels, a combination of shocking pink and electric lime green being a particular favorite, and her affinity for prints—splashy florals and small repeating motifs, like turtles, hearts, whales, crossed tennis rackets, sailboats, little maps of Nantucket, and so forth. It goes without saying that madras has always had a special place in the hearts and wardrobes of Prepettes (and those of their beaus and husbands).

Synthetic fabrics are avoided like the plague, wool and cotton being most favored

among the natural fibers. All clothing is tailored to semitailored—definitely no fuss or feathers. In truth there is a conspicuous lack of femininity in prep clothes and carriage. Monogramming of various articles of fashion is as big as the use of nicknames like Buffy, Binky and Muffy. Jewelry is kept to a minimum, but once on it never comes off. Hence you would be hard-pressed ever to find a Prepette on the tennis court without her pierced earrings. These women are very sporty, too.

The key words here are neatness, conservatism, and utility. This partial list of prep uniform staples should sum up the look for you:

Lacoste shirts
cotton turtlenecks
scoop-neck T-shirts (with piping)
men's button-down broadcloth shirts
wrap dresses and skirts
kilts
basic shirt dresses
long skirts (black velvet and plaid taffeta for dressier
    occasions)
wide-wale corduroy slacks
khakis
webbed belts
circle pins
Cartier watches on lizard bands
grosgrain ribbons
Shetland crewneck and cableknit cardigan sweaters
espadrilles, Gucci loafers, Weejuns, and Sperry
    Topsiders

After the country club years, when the predominance of gray hair can no longer be denied and grandchildren abound, the best of the Prepettes automatically and without

thought assume the look of the Old Guard. This most likely has something to do with genes.

Lessons:

1. "Uniforms" are for the most part boring and take the fun out of fashion.

2. There is no edge in looking completely unfeminine.

3. Understatement is a plus, but a little flair doesn't hurt, either.

4. Green and pink is not the most sophisticated color combination.

5. Good-quality, durable clothing lasts for years . . . and years . . . and years.

6. The sporting life is a good one.

Now, please remember that these stereotypes are just that, and like all stereotypes there are as many exceptions as there are adherents to the rule. Indeed, some of America's best-dressed women are from Dallas, and old money can be very elegant. The point of this survey is that, while other prosperous looks exist, they take a substantial amount of money to "pull off."

Timeless elegance, on the other hand, is egalitarian. It is accessible to all who care about looking terrific and who want to put together a class look without going into hock or wiping out their savings account. *Dressing Rich* will point out all the strategies and techniques and reveal all the secrets you will need to create your own million-dollar look. And only you will know how little it actually cost to do it. Without further ado, then, let's get started.

Quality

THE FIRST STEP in Dressing Rich is recognition of quality. Whether you are a legitimate heiress with unlimited funds or a hard-working woman struggling to make ends meet, you won't look monied without an awareness and appreciation of quality. No matter the price tag or label of a garment, you have to be well equipped with your own personal built-in quality detector to guarantee that you will get your money's worth and that you will recognize a genuine bargain when you see one.

Quality is a condition of excellence. In regard to fashion it means the highest standard of design, fabric and workmanship. Unfortunately, quality, in all aspects of life, is a rare commodity these days. Products are developed and marketed to appeal more to the taste of the middling mass than to the taste of the most discerning. And that, to put it simply, makes for a lot of junk out there.

If we want to look rich, our taste level has to rise above that of the masses. We have to train our senses to recognize quality and to be more discerning. Whether old or new, quality always looks rich. To quote a designer friend of mine who is a perfectionist: "Worn quality looks better and richer than perfect junk."

In her essay "The Decline of Quality" (*New York Times Magazine*, November 2, 1980), Barbara Tuchman proposes a system of "Q" and "non-Q" for defining and determining quality in all elements of our culture, from food to fine art. The system works equally well when applied to a specific field, and is an excellent basis for gauging quality in fashion.

Honesty of purpose is a criterion of Q. Above, functional, hearty Levi's worn on a ranch are very Q. Left, designer jeans that step out of the realm of the functional and pass themselves off as "legitimate fashion" are non-Q.

In the system, Q represents the works and services that have resisted mediocrity and meet two important criteria: intensive effort and honesty of purpose. Non-Q, of course, represents the opposite: those works and services that have succumbed to mediocrity.

Let's consider the concept of intensity of effort for a moment. The concentration and labor that goes into creating a fine hand-knit sweater or an impeccably tailored suit are the major elements in the garment's quality look. The same materials carelessly stitched or sloppily constructed would produce an inferior, non-Q garment. The more effort, care, and skill that combine to produce an article—from the attention to the initial fiber that yields the fabric to the sewing of the final button—the better quality the article will be.

Honesty of purpose, though a somewhat more abstract point in the fashion arena, is still applicable to some degree. "Honest" fashion is nondisputable. Functional, hearty Levi's worn on a working ranch, hiking through a forest, etc., are very Q. Designer jeans, on the other hand, which step out of the realm of the functional and pass themselves off as fashion are, in my book, strictly non-Q. Honesty, for our purposes, can also be interpreted as *the real thing*. Therefore, vinyl trimming masquerading as leather is non-Q. But plastic that loudly proclaims its "plastic-ness" could be considered Q (though never rich). You get the idea, and you can see there's lot of room for lively disagreements on just what is Q and non-Q. Since we are going to have to compromise here and there, some imitations

Plastic that makes no bones about its "plastic-ness" like the poncho on the right could be considered Q—though not necessarily rich. Plasic masquerading as leather (below) is neither Q nor rich.

are allowed, but mediocrity generally is not. If, for instance, you decide to compromise on a string of simulated pearls, they should be the best ones available—copies so excellent that even a discerning oyster couldn't tell them apart from the real thing.

Aside from the subtle distinctions of the Q system, there are some more solid guidelines for identifying quality clothes. Barring fabric and design, which will be discussed later, there are quality finishes that earmark well-made clothes and certain telltale finishings that are signs of shoddy workmanship. Unfortunately, we can't afford to be "detail fanatics" and buy only clothes that are as beautifully made on the inside as they are on the outside. But it is a good idea to be aware of quality finishing details in order to make wise investment buys and to know what to correct in moderately priced clothes.

1. Well-made garments have zippers dyed to match that are completely concealed in perfectly sewn plackets.

2. A hook and eye is the preferred

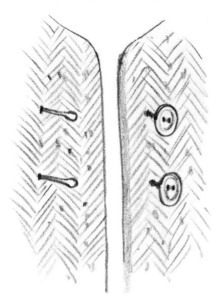

*Heavy fabrics call for
stemmed buttons.*

fastening whenever it is apt to show. You will never see a metal eye in a well-finished garment. Instead, an invisible hand-crocheted loop of thread the same color as the fabric is used.

3. Snaps are usually avoided wherever they may show. If a large snap is necessary, it should be covered with a material of the same color and, whenever possible, the same fabric as the garment.

4. No matter what buttons are made of, they should be functional. Purely decorative buttons often downgrade a garment. Matching buttons should really match (couture houses have them dyed to order). They should be stitched only through the outer layer of fabric—not through the lining. If a fabric is heavy, the button should have a "stem" that is the same thickness as the material. The stem is made by attaching the

Poorly sewn zipper   *Well sewn zipper*

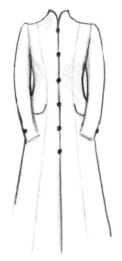

Functional buttons   *Decorative buttons*

Puckered seams make any garment look inexpensive.

button loosely, then winding the thread around between the fabric and the button. If, on the other hand, a fabric is very delicate, the underside of the spot where the button is attached should be reinforced with a small square of matching fabric and interlined with muslin if necessary.

5. Hemline stitches should be invisible from the outside of the garment. If the material is very delicate or transparent and there is no hem, the edge should be well finished by "hand rolling." Standard depth for hemlines is two inches. If you buy a garment with a poorly sewn hem, consider re-hemming before you wear it. A bad hem is a sure sign of an inexpensive garment.

6. Expensive skirts and slacks are fully lined with dyed-to-match silk, if made of wool or tweed, or with silk taffeta, if the material lacks body.

7. Seams and stitching are even and without puckers. If a seam is sewn with too wide a stitch, consider reinforcing it before wearing.

Near right, a poorly sewn hem shows. Far right, a well sewn hem is invisible.

Status Symbols

WHILE ON THE SUBJECT of quality, we should pay some attention to the question of status labels and the validity of fashion status symbols. Unfortunately, a status label no longer guarantees quality in clothing or accessories.

Before the days of *prêt à porter* (ready-to-wear), *haute couture* was an art. Designs were closely guarded until the day of the grand showing. Very few imitations were possible. Those scoundrels who did somehow manage to acquire the coveted designs and produce facsimiles never made out too well anyway—the status label simply wasn't there. In those days, the label of a top designer was indicative of quality, meaning innovative design, a made-to-order fit, the best materials and unparalleled workmanship.

Couture is rapidly dying out today. A good number of top designers have lent their names to everything from scarves to pantyhose to bedsheets and automobiles. Most items are contracted out to distant factories. Only goodwill and an occasional check by the designers' representatives guarantee the quality of whatever is being manufactured.

But that's not the worst of it. Imitations and outright counterfeits abound; designs, signatures, and trademarks are copied exactly. Although I was well aware of counterfeits, I never imagined how widespread and lucrative the imitation industry actually is until I read "The Big Couture Rip-Off" by Susan Heller Anderson in the *New York Times Magazine*. According to

There is no real status in wearing other people's initials—even if they are those of a top designer.

Anderson, $450 million in profits were reaped from bogus fashion in 1980 alone. Apparently some copies are ultimately shabby while others are quite good. She wrote, "Some fakes are so cheaply made—plastic linings, poorly sewn handles, blurred labels—that even a passing familiarity with the real article makes the difference evident. But many 'Dior' fakes are made from heavier silks. Often, Dior's people can't tell the difference."

The sources of counterfeits in this country are questionable. Some investigators suspect some organized crime involvement. Others say that most fake fashions are made by individuals within the garment industry who have been lured by the potentially huge gains.

Some fakes, though illegally imported, can be quite legally manufactured in some countries because there is at present no law that prohibits the registering of a name or trademark that belongs to a foreign firm as long as it has not been registered in the country of the imitation's entrepreneur. Designers are understandably outraged by this. Pierre Cardin, for one, was openly critical of the South Korean government after a visit to Seoul in 1978: "I saw my name and initials on the most shoddy products, from T-shirts to sneakers and on things having nothing to do with the name Cardin. It is scandalous that a government should allow this." To protect themselves from this sort of "legal" pirating, firms now frequently register trademarks and designs in countries where they have no intention of marketing their goods.

Designers and designs that have been imitated read like a fashion encyclopedia: Saint Laurent, Hermes, Chanel, Cartier, Louis Vuitton, Courrèges, Dior, Gucci, Céline, Cardin, and many, many others. The legitimate fashion industry is fighting back. Cartier, for instance, spends one million dollars annually on warning advertisements in trade publications, investigations, and prosecutions aimed at thwarting counterfeiting. Yet, I have a feeling that the counterfeit fashion trade will be as hard to subdue as the drug trade. If there is a demand for a product and there's money to be made in supplying it, it will be produced.

This predicament is not as unfortunate for you as it is for the fashion industry. The main point is that you can't judge an article by label alone. The status of the fashion status symbol is on the wane. Wearing a Cartier tank watch or carrying a Vuitton bag, to name two of the omnipresent prestige items, doesn't automatically mean you have money. You don't need a lot to own an imitation, and you often would be hard put to tell the difference.

The equalizer is taste. If you honestly like the look and/or the qualities of a "status symbol," by all means buy it and wear it proudly. But if you are buying strictly for status—don't.

Quantity

THE NEXT MAJOR consideration is quantity. There are two quantitative factors involved in Dressing Rich. The first is wardrobe size, the second, moderation. The bottom line is always *less quantity, more quality*. The truth is that you simply don't need a myriad of clothes to look rich. A small, flexible, select wardrobe composed of top-quality apparel is one-hundred times more effective—and easier to manage—than a colossal collection of mediocre clothing.

You don't need a new and different ensemble for each day of the year, or even for each day of the week. It's not a stigma to be seen in the same outfit more than once, even if you are constantly in the public eye. If anything, it is a demonstration of self-confidence, security and fashion wisdom. Our First Lady has my unqualified respect in this regard. She buys wisely (no matter how much money she may spend on a particular dress) and unabashedly gets full mileage out of her clothes. *Women's Wear Daily*, which religiously records Nancy Reagan's public appearances, has commented benignly on her "seven-year-old Jean Louis dress" and her "well-traveled green tunic" by designer Bill Blass.

This principle, which would be called "austerity chic," has been practiced by elegant French women for years. Austerity is slowly but surely influencing the American fashion scene, in light of tighter times. It is always wiser to invest in a small, quality wardrobe now that will see you gracefully through the lean years, when and if they

Simplicity is the key to chic. The look on the left will always be in style. The one on the right will always be questionable.

come, and that can be inexpensively augmented. Why not look rich—even in a faltering economy?

The second quantitative factor involves moderation. Anything—regardless of cost—worn in excess looks terribly tacky and negates a monied look. Simplicity is the key to chic. "Less is more" is definitely the rule. You'll never look richer by adding more and more. One carefully selected dinner ring, for example, is a much better bet than a combination of three bracelets, a necklace, earrings, brooch, and a beaded bag, even if they are each worth a king's ransom.

Wearing too much jewelry is a common blunder and smacks of the arriviste. One of the real pleasures of being truly rich (or so I've been told) is that you don't have to prove it, especially by flashing the family jewels. Flashy is very déclassé.

The important point here is that too much of anything can spell disaster: too much fur, too many ruffles, too much detail, or too much makeup. Excess not only looks lowbrow, but it distracts from your own personal style. Your fashion should enhance your natural charm and beauty—not steal its thunder. Garbo, Hepburn, Dietrich, and the other legendary beauties of our time are not remembered for their flounces and baubles but for their purity of beauty, their simplicity of style, and their uniqueness.

Enough said. Keep the lines clean and the accessories simple and you've got half the battle won.

Investment Buying

IT GOES WITHOUT SAYING that wise allocation of wardrobe funds is crucial when working within a limited budget. Clothing investments should be thought out as clearly as stock investments in order to reap good, steady, long-term rewards. Here the dividends come in the form of clothing performance and chic. The better your investments the more self-confidence, elegance and overall chic you'll radiate. And the wiser the investments the longer the dividends will pay off.

Good investment buys are very select and special pieces that are quintessentially you. They are perfectly suited to your lifestyle, and have the potential of becoming old, faithful allies. For example, such irreplaceable and priceless items as an impeccably tailored, classic tweed jacket that looks as if it were made for you and goes with everything in your closet, or a luxuriously soft, steel-blue cashmere scarf that matches the color of your eyes and makes them seem to sparkle would have to be considered excellent investment buys—no matter what you had to pay for them.

You can't expect every clothing purchase to be a great investment buy, but when you spend a substantial amount on an item—say over $75—it should be a piece with a future, not just a one-night (or one-month) stand.

There are five inherent aspects to a given garment or accessory that can classify it as an investment buy:

1. Excellent quality
2. Classic design

3. Flexibility: as a basic foundation piece for your wardrobe

4. Durability, which provides longevity

5. Comfort and a flattering fit.

If a potential purchase can meet at least four of these standards your money will be well spent.

Investment buys add up over the years and

are the understructure of a successful, classy wardrobe. It's smart to make one of these special additions whenever you can afford it—a great jacket here, a wonderful scarf there, a cashmere sweater, and so on. They are like money in the bank.

Still, don't get too carried away with investment buys. You do have to be sensible when it gets down to money. I was recently looking to invest in a pair of lightweight wool khaki slacks that would be suitable for every season, except the dead heat of summer. I found the exact classic style I was looking for at the Yves Saint Laurent boutique for a walloping $365. Needless to say, I moved on. Spending that kind of money on a pair of simple wool slacks is insane, even if they are perfect. After some serious shopping, I found the slacks I was looking for. They were the same fabric as the others. The cut and styling were just as good, and they were $90, which is at least a reasonable price for a garment that I will wear for years.

It is especially important to comparison-shop when there is a considerable outlay of money involved. If you see something you like but feel you might be able to get the same quality for less, ask the salesperson to hold it for you while you complete your shopping expedition. Most will be happy to comply. It's a good idea to get her name and telephone number and to call her at the end of the day to let her know your intentions. That way you can always go back the next day and pick up your first choice if you haven't found anything better or less expensive.

Fads, Trends, and the Classics

FADDISH OR TRENDY CLOTHES fall terribly short of being any sort of an investment buy. Beware of this common pitfall. Spending a lot of hard-earned cash on cute, trendy items is sheer foolishness. Unlike "legitimate" fashion, which is influenced by and is a reflection of socioeconomic conditions, trends and fads are most often spawned by either a big, immediate push from the fashion industry or a highly publicized media event like a movie. *Tom Jones*, *Doctor Zhivago*, *Annie Hall*, and *Urban Cowboy* are a few examples of cinematic influence. Fussy, ruffled country-squire blouses from Fielding's England; midi-length skirts with boots, cossack shirts, fox-trimmed coats from Tsarist Russia; sloppy, oversized jackets and vests, ties, men's hats, and frizzy hair from Woody Allen's New York; and full Western get-ups direct from Gilley's in Texas have all had their moments in the fashion sun. Trends are very "of the moment." Although some can be quite fetching and creative, they do not withstand the trials of time. Some designs actually are so ephemeral that by the time you get them back from their first visit to the cleaners they are utterly démodé.

Another drawback to trends and fads is that they carry overtones of what *Women's Wear Daily* has dubbed the "Fashion Victim," a death knell for elegance and haute society. An FV is naively showy as opposed to coolly classic. To look rich there should be no implication whatsoever that you are trying to impress anyone. Again, and I can't mention this enough, it's always better to be safe and classic rather than overly fashionable and sorry.

Some of the more unappealing faddish items that I have noted within the last few years are the jumpsuit, which is at its best when being dropped from an airplane; high-heeled backless sandals, which are especially tacky when worn with tight jeans or bathing suits and would make even Snow White look like she came from the wrong side of the tracks; Jellies, the clear plastic flat shoes, which sound and look as if they should not be worn but eaten; and the newly revised

Movie fads: Opposite left, the Tom Jones *look; near right,* Dr. Zhivago; *far right,* Annie Hall.

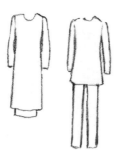

jodhpur pants, which look chic only atop an English saddle. There are, of course, many more, but you get the idea. Simply remember that the rich are never in the fashion forefront. They neither set nor follow trends. They stick within the realm of the classics.

And classics are fashion perennials, sometimes with a slightly new variation on the theme. Line and design are simple and neat. Materials are of top quality, fine and durable. The colors are largely neutral. The shirtwaist dress, the dirndl skirt, the Chanel slingback shoe, the French beret, a string of pearls, the tunic top, the turtleneck sweater, and the straight-legged, tailored, pleated trouser, for instance, are all time-tested fashion classics.

Most likely you'll be able to think of women you know who step beyond the parameters of the classics and still manage to look splendidly elegant and rich. Chances are that these women are one of two things: either they are indeed very rich, or they are very creative.

The very affluent can easily afford to hire someone with exquisite taste to help them shape their wardrobes. They are in the enviable position of being able to commission top designers to design clothes specifically for them—and for every occasion. With the

guidance of top experts in every fashion-related field—design, hair, makeup, nutrition, and exercise—wealthy women can afford to be more adventurous.

Especially creative women with great personal style, flair, or presence can be even more adventurous, and without any counseling. No rules needed here. These women, either directly or indirectly, are usually involved in fashion or some facet of the arts. Dame Edith Sitwell, Kay Thompson, Louise Nevelson and Paloma Picasso, to name a few, have managed to establish a reputation for personal elegance with occasionally extreme dress styles. Dame Edith Sitwell, for instance, often wore cowled headpieces, gold brocade robes, and huge jet and ivory rings. Instead of trying to camouflage her extraordinary height (six feet) and Byzantine looks with ordinary clothes, she made the best of what she had by turning herself into something marvelously gothic. The look is not for many.

Individualism of this kind is very uncommon, but if you've got the personality, creativity, and rare presence to carry off a wonderful, exotic look all your own, you have my wholehearted approval to go for it.

Dame Edith Sitwell

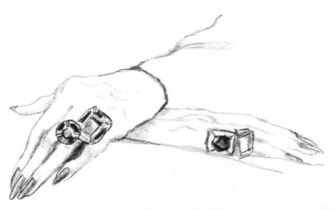

Grooming

PERSONAL GROOMING is one of those things that is too easy to overlook, especially when you are constantly on the run. But its importance should never be underestimated. There is no way to look rich, successful, elegant, or even pleasantly stylish if your grooming isn't up to snuff. Bad grooming can turn a silk purse into a sow's ear in a flash.

Grooming, as a legitimate fashion concept, seems to have gone the way of fussy white gloves and pillbox hats. The word itself is almost an anachronism. Perhaps it's because we have become so sophisticated and liberated that some would consider a mere mention of the merits of personal hygiene somewhat condescending at best, and an affront to our new-found freedom at worst. But it is because we are so liberated, and our lives so active, that basic self-maintenance has slipped unnoticed to a low position on our priority list.

Crinolines and Merry Widow corsets may be démodé, but personal upkeep is still a mainstay of good fashion. I have heard it said that "soap is the cornerstone of elegance." That might be pushing it a bit: being well-scrubbed, shampooed, and pressed doesn't automatically lead to elegance. If that were the case, there would be a minimum of three registered nurses on the best-dressed list every year. Still, it is a key component of looking one's best.

It's no wonder that flawless grooming is practically synonymous with looking well-to-do. Weekly hair appointments, manicures, pedicures, facials, waxings, mud baths, new and assorted "wonder" treatments, personal maids, and so on make it marvelously easy for our fortunate sisters to keep their act together. Don't despair, though—it's not all that difficult for us either. Granted, "do-it-yourself" home care is not as much fun, but it is easily accomplished. We simply have to donate more time and energy to the cause. The way I look at it, a little extra effort is not a stiff price to pay for a key aspect of a class look.

The worst transgressions, such as dirty hair, stained clothing, fallen hems, dandruff-dusted shoulders are, needless to say, anathema. But even lesser offenses can make a sizable difference to your impression on others. Something as seemingly minor as nail care can tell as much about your station in life as your clothes. A recent personal experience is a good case in point.

Last fall, on one of those perfect, brisk sunny days that make living in the Northeast worthwhile, I was riding my bike (the only totally independent form of transportation in New York) to an interview near Central Park. When I realized that I was early, I sat down on the nearest bench and took a big breath of rare unpolluted air. A prosperous-looking middle-aged man, who shared my bench, interrupted my thoughts with a comment on the magnificently colored leaves. The ensuing conversation was pleasant and rather routine. Since my mind was occupied with the issue of first impressions and the importance thereof, I redirected the course of the talk. This, I had realized, was a perfect test situation. We were complete strangers without known common interests or shared business or social

Watch out for hanging coat linings.

Baggy pantyhose should definitely be avoided.

ties. We agreed to exchange first impressions. I could tell him what I figured was his position in society—age, career, income, etc.—and he would estimate mine.

I was sure I had an edge since I wasn't exactly at my most chic: black sweatpants, red sweatshirt over an ancient black turtleneck sweater, red running shoes, and blue and red reversible down vest. My bike and knapsack were run-of-the-mill. Nothing on or about me was costly. The only possible clue to my involvement with fashion was a conspicuous lack thereof.

The results of this extemporaneous experiment were amazing. We were both right on target. He even mentioned fashion as one of my four probable careers. He estimated my salary as higher than it unfortunately is. "I look at the hands first," said the admitted corporate lawyer. "If the hands are well cared for, it's upper income. If they're a mess, it's lower. I knew where you were coming from before you spoke word one." He went on to explain that even though a sweatshirt per se is questionable in his opinion, a clean one isn't. My color combination, he said, was rather sophisticated, "artsy," so I had to be somehow related to fashion or the arts. An interesting chance encounter.

"My hands!" I thought. "I must remember to keep them in good shape. Who would have thought a lawyer would even notice my nails?"

With the importance of being well groomed in mind, then, let the following hints serve as a refresher and checklist.

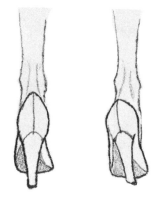

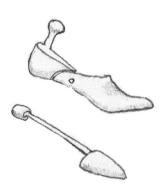

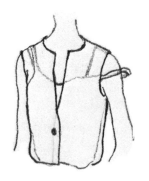

• Shoes should be clean, well polished, and well heeled. It's a good idea to use a little preventive medicine and have plastic heel protectors put on expensive shoes that you expect to wear frequently.

• Suede shoes should be revived with a suede brush after wearing, and patent leather will shine like new after a quick wipe with Windex.

• It is recommended that you alternate shoes to give both the shoes and your feet a rest.

• Shoes will last longer and look better if you put shoe trees in them when not in use.

• Pantyhose with baggy knees and/or runs are to be avoided at all cost. It's a good idea to have an extra pair on hand. Pantyhose is one item that you can spend less money on and still get quality. Super-market pantyhose are a good bet if you are a daily wearer.

• Hemlines should be invisible and even all around, with no slip or linings hanging below. A poorly sewn hem can sometimes give away the price of an inexpensive garment. It may be worth your while to undo these hems (which are sometimes machine-stitched) and re-hem them your-self using a blind stitch.

• Underwear should never be seen, either in outline form through sheer material or by straps peeking out from bare dresses. If straps are a problem, try sewing in small strap holders to wide-necked or sleeveless dresses.

• Coat linings have a tendency to drop after

much wear. Check frequently and re-hem when necessary.

• If you have a tendency to perspire, consider using dress shields, especially when wearing silk. There is a vast variety to choose from, including stick-on disposable ones.

• Overstarching and fold lines are the stamp of the Chinese laundry syndrome. If you use Chinese laundries or others with the same effect, request no starch and that the garments be hung on hangers.

• Perfume can be a wonderful signature but it should never be used in excess. (The sensibilities of others should be considered.)

• Hands should always be well kept and the nails well manicured. Chipped nail polish should be tended to immediately. Obviously, nails that are bitten, too long, or polished with an unnatural color like violet are positive taboos.

• Proper pressing of garments is imperative.

• Clothes will look fresher and last longer if hung on soft or contour hangers. Wire hangers often leave lines and sometimes ruin the drape of a garment.

• Dark wools should be brushed or mitted with a lint mitt to remove any lint.

• Silver, brass, or other metal details on accessories like handbags should be kept free of tarnish.

Since makeup and hair are such crucial elements of a polished turnout, we will cover them individually in Chapter 4.

2

THE PRINCIPLES: THE BASIC TENETS OF RICH DRESSING

Design,
Color,
Fabric

EVERY SEASON the stores are filled with an exciting array of new fashions. They can be enticing, alluring, fun to look at—and often downright confusing. How do you know which of the new offerings will be good investments and will provide lasting elegance? Which garments will withstand the trial of time and not look outdated by the next season?

The answer is easy. Every garment is made up of three major components: design, color, and fabric. For a particular item to look rich and elegant each of these ingredients has to unite in perfect harmony and meet some specific standards. If all the parts are choice and work well together, the whole will be a garment that's a winning purchase. If they fall short, the garment should be questioned, for its elegance is not guaranteed. It is rather like a gourmet recipe: if you don't use just the right ingredients, the dish won't be as tasty. Let's look at these ingredients one at a time and discuss the high standards of classic chic.

Design

MOST OF the designs presented each season will be outmoded before the year is out. Every once in a while, perhaps twice a decade, a classic will be created in clothes and accessories, the silhouette of which will not only greatly affect current fashion, but will reappear in various incarnations time and time again. Some examples: The Chanel suit, the chemise, the tunic, the "costume" (a simple straight dress with its own jacket), the blazer, the Chanel two-toned shoe, the espadrille, the casual moccasin or loafer, and so on.

Simplicity, clarity of shape, and clean lines indicate a classic, timeless, and rich-looking design. There is good reason why the classics these days are such studies in simplicity, lacking much extra detail. At the same time

The shirtwaist dress

The blazer

The double cape

that fashion became less exclusive and available to the growing middle class the era of underpaid skilled labor was coming to an end. The production of high-quality, lavish trimmings like lace and embroidery, fine detailing, and intricate cut was slowly becoming a lost art. Designers and manufacturers took the only logical direction—they turned to simpler designs

The Chanel suit

The '20s chemise

that took less skill to produce. At this point, one most often has a choice between simplicity or poor detailing. I strongly suggest selecting the former.

Some of the most creative designers today eliminate all nonessential structural details. They avoid traditional shoulder seams, darts, or straight sleeves and reduce the design to a pure shape. These designs are the essence of simplicity. Ronaldus Shamask, one of the new "architects of fashion," speaks of his designs as "a kind of elegant but complicated simplicity one might find in a Ming vase."

Aside from basic simplicity, there are some fundamental design principles you should understand in order to choose the most flattering lines and shapes for you. No matter how much money you spend, if the basic design is not personally becoming, you won't look your best. Once these principles become an automatic and subconscious part of your fashion vocabulary, shopping will seem easier as decisions become quicker and mistakes less frequent.

Line

THE FIRST DESIGN principle is line, which is often used synonymously with style. A garment basically has three major sets of lines that establish shapes, influence the mood, and affect the eye movement of the beholder: body lines, silhouette lines, and detail lines. (If the fabric has a pattern, another set of lines is created.)

The body lines are created by the seams, darts, tucks, etc., that provide the contour and fit the garment to your body. The silhouette line is formed by the basic shape of the garment. Here, for example, are a few basic silhouette lines:

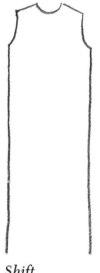

Shift

A-line   *Blouson*   *Princess*   *Shirtwaist*

Detail lines

Since our eyes are naturally conditioned to follow the direction that we read—from left to right and from top to bottom—if all is equal we will more readily follow a horizontal line than a vertical one. By clever placement and direction of dominant lines we can redirect the eye to suit our purpose. A particular line will become dominant if it is wider, brighter, longer, or repeated more often than another.

The eye also follows a straight line more directly and rapidly, while it moves slowly along a curved line. Thus a garment made up of only straight lines will appear more architectural and severe—like the very geometric high fashions of Courrèges and Rudi Gernreich that were so popular in the sixties. A garment created with curved lines will present a more relaxed, graceful, and softer look.

With these rules in mind it is easy to use lines to create illusions. Needless to say,

these illusions should work for you, not
against. Remember that no fashion "rules" are
hard and fast. The effect of several related
lines is invariably greater than that of one. So
you don't have to avoid all "unflattering
lines"; just don't let them be the dominant
ones.

In order to use line to your best advantage
you have to take an objective and realistic
look at your body and decide what you would
like to conceal and what you would like to
emphasize, then put one of the following
lines to work to draw the eye of the viewer
just where you want it.

VERTICALS

VERTICAL LINES, in fabric patterns, detailing,
or basic silhouette, will make you appear
taller and thinner as they lead the eye up and

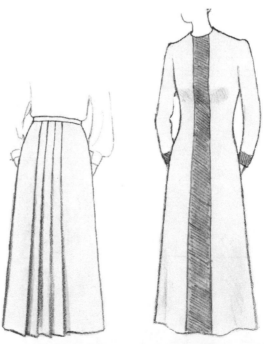

*Solid color, near right, creates
stronger impression of height.*

down. V-necks, shawl collars, shoulder to
hemline seams, and pleats are some examples
of vertical lines. Single vertical lines give the
strongest impression of height. If there are
several vertical lines repeated at intervals
across the garment, the illusion of length will
be slightly diffused because the eye will tend
to move horizontally as well as vertically.

Straight or long silhouettes that are
unbroken by contrasting colors also create a
vertical line that will add to the illusion of
height.

HORIZONTALS

HORIZONTAL LINES, of course, emphasize width—especially when two or more are used together. You can, however, sometimes create an impression of length with a horizontal line if you place it above or below the middle of your body, since then it will make one section look unusually long. At all costs avoid placing a strong horizontal line in an unflattering place, especially across the hips.

DIAGONALS

THE EFFECT of diagonal lines depends primarily on the angle and the length of the line. A short diagonal will give the impression of width by leading the eye sideways, while a long diagonal will give a narrower and longer impression by leading the eye downward as well as across.

Diane Von Furstenburg's asymmetrical wrap dress is a good example of a long diagonal line. Diagonals can be rather effective, because they can accomplish the same thing as a straight line but are softer and less severe.

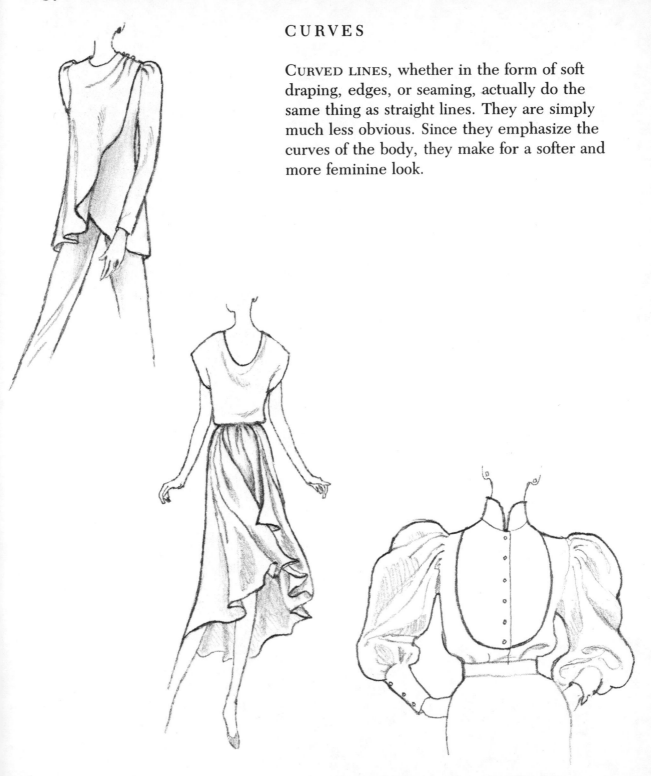

CURVES

CURVED LINES, whether in the form of soft draping, edges, or seaming, actually do the same thing as straight lines. They are simply much less obvious. Since they emphasize the curves of the body, they make for a softer and more feminine look.

Of the lines we've discussed, it's impossible to say that one is richer looking than another. The elegance comes from the way they work in relationship to your body and the way they are used within a particular design. The best and most sophisticated designs make optimum use of a minimum of lines. Just as a fine artist may need only a few expert strokes of the brush to render a perfect likeness of form, a good designer needs only a few lines to create a winning garment.

Certain silhouettes are more in tune with the times than others. Today, although shapes and styles are quite varied, the general silhouette is one of ease, comfort, and fluidity. A stiff, close, precise silhouette, like the A-line dress for instance, looks outdated. It is not necessary to follow fashion's every move, but it is important to be aware of its general mood and directions.

With today's emphasis on comfort and fluidity, the dress at the left looks current, while the stiff A-line dress on the right looks as outdated as it is.

Proportion

PROPORTION IS the other major design element that we must consider. Most clothes on the market today are intrinsically well-designed. The question to be answered is: for whom? Each person's body has a slightly different set of proportions. Even if you are the exact height and weight as someone else, chances are that your proportions aren't the same: your hips may be a little wider, your legs a bit longer, your neck a little shorter, shoulders a touch wider, and so on. Hence, a design that is perfect for one woman might be less than satisfactory for another. Unless you are one of the rare and lucky ones to be blessed with a perfectly proportioned model's figure, you have to look for clothes and accessories whose proportions are in harmony with your own. Any of you who have neglected the proportion factor and have bought particular fashions because they've looked great on your best friend or on a model in a magazine have already learned this lesson the hard way.

Proportion is a simple but subtle matter of interdependent space/size relationships. In fashion this means that if you make one section of your body look longer, wider, or larger, another section will appear shorter, narrower, or smaller. For example a pair of high-waisted slacks with a cummerbund-type waistline will make your legs appear longer—and your torso shorter. And a long jacket with shoulder pads will make your torso appear longer and broader, while your lower body will look shorter and smaller.

Through clever use of line, color and texture, you can shift your "natural balance"

and create a new sense of proportion by emphasizing your positive features and lessening attention on your negative ones: you can broaden or narrow shoulders, lengthen or shorten the waist, make yourself appear shorter or taller. Color can be used in much the same way—it can accent one feature and subordinate another. A white scarf, for example, worn with a solid navy shift will draw the eye up to the neck and face and away from the hips, waist, and legs. Take the scarf away, and the eye will be drawn to the waist first.

Texture influences proportion because of its bulk or lack of it. A heavy cableknit sweater is obviously going to make your torso appear larger than one made of lightweight cashmere.

The subtleties of line and proportion are often hard to spot, but once you are aware of them and how they are created, you are already ahead of the game. To further train your eye, study store windows, fashion magazines and people on the street, and try to figure out why a particular outfit looks balanced or unbalanced. Don't feel foolish practicing in front of a mirror. It is one of the best ways to tune your eye. Experiment with different combinations, hem lengths, and accessories, and objectively question if the lines of the garment are in proportion to your body shape. Ask also if the color, details and textures, and widths and lengths are related, and if the accessories are too large or too small, too delicate or too massive within the context of a particular ensemble.

With a new awareness and a little practice

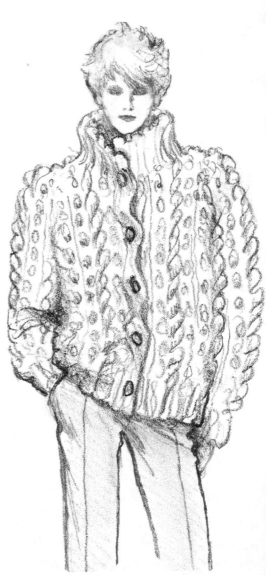

Opposite left, a long jacket makes the legs appear shorter; a short jacket adds length to the legs. Above, a white scarf worn with a dark outfit will draw the eye to the face; a white belt worn with the same outfit will draw attention to the waist. Right, the texture of this cable-knit sweater adds extra dimension to the upper body.

you will be able to master these proportion details that make for a well-balanced, sophisticated, and elegant fashion look.

Color

IF LINE AND PROPORTION are the most subtle fashion factors we have to consider, color is the most obvious. Its impact should never be underestimated. Anyone—unschooled, uninterested, and unaware of the fine points and esoteric nuances of high fashion though they may be—will react (whether consciously or not) to the colors you are wearing. Wear all whites and you are fresh, pure, summery, and cool. Wear all red and you are racy and dynamic. All black: you are demure, quietly sexy, and slightly mysterious. The more subtle the colors and the color combinations, the less aware people will be of the influence the colors have on them. But they will be affected whether or not they realize it.

Not only can skillful use of color help you create the image you would like to project, but it can also help you save money. You can wear moderately priced or friendly, old, high-quality clothes and blend the colors so expertly that the final composite outfit will look much richer than its parts.

This is one of my favorite ploys. I always find it immensely satisfying to find myself at an exclusive social gathering looking as chic as the select, affluent guests around me (and, I might humbly add, occasionally more so)—and at considerably less expense.

Only last month color came to my rescue again. I was invited to a friend's garden wedding reception. She is from a very Old Guard, very wealthy family. So even though

she assured me that the dress was quite casual, I figured there were bound to be some ancient diamonds and chiffon gracing the grounds. "Casual," after all, in some circles means no tails or black tie. On the other hand, since my friend was a former hippie (albeit with blue-blood credentials) I didn't want to overdo it, either. And I should add that I was neither in the mood nor financial situation to do any fancy shopping.

The old color ploy, I concluded half-consciously, as I surveyed my meager, wanting wardrobe. Since a wedding is a happy occasion, I ruled out black. Whites would do the trick. After trying on and analyzing every conceivable combination my closet could offer, including, for the sake of objectivity, a few other color mixes, I settled on a pair of white cotton pleated slacks (only one year old), a light cream, softly draped silk blouse (only two years old), a white, slightly full, dropped-sleeve cotton jacket (Calvin Klein, circa 1976—untouched and unappreciated since 1978), a string of pearls (a touch of tradition), classy beige shoes, medium heel (just a few months old), and an old, friendly, and omnipresent beige belt with a gold buckle (still classy after all these years). I popped up the collars of the shirt and jacket, rolled the cream silk cuffs over the sleeves of the white jacket, and off I went—a vision in white. Who would notice details when confronted by a personification of freshness, cleanliness, and the spirit of summer?

The result? I had interpreted "casual" correctly. More than half of the guests were in fact more formally dressed than I, but I was not underdressed. Even a few of the "chiffons" told me how wonderful I looked, and "so cool on such a hot day."

Now, I admit that the silk shirt and the pearls were a contributing factor to my gracious acceptance to the "inside"—and, I might add, to my resulting peace of mind. But it was the color that created a slightly more formal image. The unity of color played down each individual piece of the outfit and produced a strong overall impression. Had the jacket or slacks been another color, I would not have looked as "dressed," and each piece of the outfit would have had to be a gem and be able to stand up on its own.

To regress for just a minute, a major point that I made earlier is also well illustrated here. If you want to save money, remember that versatility is more important than quantity. Each piece of my ensemble, as it were, is extremely flexible and makes for very different looks when worn with other separates and accessories. "Maximum use of minimum goods" is an idea worth remembering.

Monochromatic outfits, with slight variations in tone (like my reception garb), will look most sophisticated in neutral tones like white, black (especially), and beige (the favorite of Marlene Dietrich). Although other monochromatic schemes can work, you will find that most other colors profit by a subtle blending with another color, especially with one of the same value. We'll get to that in a minute, but first we need to talk about choosing the "right" colors.

If my attention seems focused primarily on neutrals, it is for good reason. The fashion neutrals—beiges, tans, taupe, grays, black, whites, and navy—are the key colors in our Dressing Rich scheme. These colors, and their wide variety of shades and tones, are fashion perennials. They will never be unfashionable. They will always appear elegant. And they are extremely versatile. Your choice of these reliable, classic colors should constitute the framework of your wardrobe. Choose colors that are most flattering to your skin tone and personal coloring. There are shades among these "primary rich colors" that will be complimentary to every complexion. If, for instance, you have a very pale complexion and find black to be draining, concentrate on the beige family. Greige—a combination of gray and beige—looks exceptionally well on light blondes, and is a consummate "rich neutral." If you have an olive complexion, avoid any of the beiges with yellow undertones. Select instead any of the other neutrals, with off-white and black being particularly flattering choices. Auburn hair? Try, among others, one of the deeper shades of tan, like chestnut. A wardrobe based on any of the primary rich neutrals will be a winning one. And a classic, neutral color will further insure the longevity and value of any investment buy.

Now, there are a few rare people who live quite happily in neutrals alone, and there are even some, like Yoko Ono, who have made those colors a part of their personal signature. We too could put together a chic—albeit

Beige shoes and bag will always look chic with the beige suit, no matter what color blouse you wear with it.

stylized—neutral wardrobe. But most of us crave a bit more variety. And so to your neutral foundation you can add your choice of the "secondary rich colors."

These secondary colors leave a little more room for adventure: deep burgundy, red, plum, dusty gray/green, Confederate and slate blue, and soft, dusty, muted pastels. This color group is also relatively timeless, sophisticated, and classy. But because they make a much more definite color statement (the true neutrals are almost an absence of color), they are less flexible, more difficult to mix and match, and require more specialized accessories. Therefore, when money is an issue, they are impractical as foundation colors. But they are wonderfully effective, when blended with the neutrals, in adding interest, variety and color sophistication to various ensembles. Again consider which shades are most flattering to your individual coloring. Then integrate your choice of secondary colors into your neutral foundation.

There are other colors, such as turquoise, emerald green, bright blue, and purple that can be worn effectively by some women, but because they make such an appreciable statement of their own, they have to be especially well suited to the individual and of superior design to look at all elegant. These colors are, in short, not a sure bet. They could look great, but then again, they could miss by a mile. If you have a proclivity to one of these "borderline" colors and feel very confident about your color sense, don't deny yourself on my account. But if you are at all unsure you might as well stick with a sure

The same suit in any secondary color would call for specific color accessorizing to look its best.

thing and follow the prescribed color plan.

A few colors are guaranteed to miss by considerably more than a mile, for they are the antithesis of elegance and should be avoided at all costs. They are mustard yellow, orange, lime green, and magenta. Anyone who can look chic in these colors should be listed in *Ripley's Believe It or Not*. I have no rational explanation for my aversion to these colors other than the experience of never seeing them look anything but awful.

Our compact color plan makes mixing and matching easy and leaves little room for error. Almost all the secondary shades blend well with the primaries, and all the primaries are complementary to each other. Color balance is the only thing that requires a bit more consideration. While there are no hard and fast color composition rules for fashion, there are some color balances that are best bets for assuring elegance:

1. Use a primary neutral as the predominant color of a particular outfit when blending with a secondary color. For example, a beige wool skirt worn with a soft plum silk blouse and a beige cashmere cardigan. The secondary color, plum, is subordinated by the primary beige. If the situation were reversed and plum the predominant color, you would have to find shoes, bag, and other accessories to perfectly complement the plum. Your basic beige shoes wouldn't do the trick—the outfit would look unbalanced. Unless you can afford a special set of accessories for each ensemble, keep the neutrals predominant and use the secondary colors for interest. You will always look chic

Yes

No

with your outfit in perfect balance.

2. When mixing either primaries alone or with secondary colors, it's a good idea to keep the darker shade on the bottom. The reverse can work quite well, but because the bottom half is proportionately larger, it is more difficult to achieve a pleasing balance. A white blouse and a black skirt, for instance, provides a more pleasing proportion than a white skirt and a black blouse. You could, however, shift the balance by adding a white accent to the top section—a scarf, a cardigan. The closer in value the colors of the top and bottom the less this rule applies. (Value is the lightness or darkness of a color.)

3. Mixing colors of the same value is a favorite device of top designers and makes for some especially sophisticated blends. A pair of classic gray flannel slacks, for example, would look quite chic when worn with a silk shirt in dusty slate blue, muted gray green, medium tan or a deep dusty rose. The effect would be quite ordinary and less interesting if the blouse colors were simple, light, pure pastels.

PLAIDS, PRINTS AND OTHER PATTERNS

PRINTS, plaids, and other patterns can be sparsely integrated into your wardrobe but should ultimately be subtle and in the same color families we have already discussed. A very fine blue pinstripe on a beige or cream background, an understated madras plaid, or a tiny wine print on a black background, for example, would all be good choices.

Understatement is the key word when it comes to plaids (left) and stripes (right).

No   Yes

The key word here is understatement. Once a pattern starts to make a statement by and of itself, it is going to adversely affect the total impression. Splashy prints, wide colorful stripes, and loud plaids should not even be in your fashion vocabulary.

Even when patterns do meet our standards it's not advisable to overstock them or to overindulge your desires for them. They are, in the long run, less versatile in mixing and matching, tend to be recalled by the viewer longer, and cannot be as easily rejuvenated with new and interesting accessories as solids can. Also, since designers rarely use a particular print more than one season, patterned garments are more easily dated.

In conclusion, let me here give a brief recap of the advantages of our fine color system.

No   *Yes*

Extravagant floral patterns are better suited for kitchen wallpaper than for dresses.

1. The colors are so classic and basic that you can wear them forever without ever worrying whether or not they are "in fashion." They always will be. And they will always be elegant.

2. In the long run it will be much less expensive to put your wardrobe together. Since all the colors are more or less seasonless, you will have many crossover items that will be suitable for two or more seasons. You'll simply need fewer clothes.

3. Your basic accessories can be kept to a minimum since you won't need a different selection for each outfit. Everything will tend to go together. Again, you've saved money.

4. Shopping will be easier and will take less time. By using color as a major criterion, you can breeze through the store and stop to investigate only when the right color attracts your eye. This saves a lot of physical and mental energy as well as time.

Fabric

THERE IS no question that some fabrics look and feel richer than others. Fine silks and cashmere, for example, just seem to exude money. Doubleknit polyesters, on the other hand, do not. With fabrics the Q and non-Q classification system again enters the picture. A lot of time, effort, and skilled labor goes into creating top-quality fabrics. Just think how many industrious little silkworms it takes to spin enough silk for just one luxurious silk blouse—not to mention the refining and weaving processes involved. Or consider how many goats have to be bred, fed, and shorn to produce a full-fashioned cashmere coat. No polyester-producing creatures need be cared for to create a doubleknit.

A fabric that requires a tremendous amount of time, care, and expertise during the various stages of its production will naturally be more expensive than one that is comparatively uncomplicated to create. Hence the high cost not only of fine silks and cashmeres, but of quality wools and linens, the specialty fibers such as vicuña, camel's hair and alpaca, and top-grade leathers and suedes.

In the long run, keeping our "investment buy" standards for color and design, it pays to invest in at least a few garments made of the highest caliber fabrics, and especially wools, where quality variances are easily discernible. Superior fabrics not only have an undeniable, exclusive, class look, but most are extremely durable. If treated with respect and properly maintained, they will probably last as long as you do. A wonderful English tweed jacket, an exquisitely draped silk charmeuse blouse, or a full cashmere shawl, for instance, will always look incredibly elegant and opulent—this year or fifteen years from now. The investment value is real.

There are, of course, plenty of other fabrics aside from the highest-priced luxury ones that have a quality look and are perfectly acceptable on the Dressing Rich plan. The real issue at hand is whether to side with the purists (most notably the Prepettes) who remain one-hundred-percent faithful to the four natural fibers—wool, cotton, linen, and silk—and who cringe at the idea of allowing a man-made fiber to touch their bodies, or to join the ranks of the radical opposition, who consider synthetics to be a very viable alternative. Ultimately the decision is a very subjective one and is entirely up to you. While I personally lean to the right and prefer the tried-and-true naturals, the fact cannot be overlooked that synthetics have come a long way. The best of the lot are quite good and are responsible for some very attractive fabrics. They have the main advantage of easy maintenance, but, on the other hand, they don't "breathe" well, often have a lot of static electricity, and are not usually as durable as the natural fibers. Again, you have to establish your personal priorities. A wardrobe that includes a few synthetics is fine, but I can guarantee that a wardrobe consisting of nothing but can never be truly an elegant one.

The most important thing to keep in mind if you do decide to incorporate some synthetics into your wardrobe is that they were originally designed to simulate the natural fibers, and to look rich they must do that, and do it very well indeed. They should be faithful replicas of their natural counterparts. If the naked eye cannot distinguish them from the real McCoy, they may certainly be considered possibilities. If they shout their chemical origin, forget them. That, of course, immediately rules out flimsy nylons, tacky polyester doubleknits and the like.

There are also a multitude of natural/synthetic blends on the market. Good blends are perfectly acceptable as well, again providing that they have the appearance of fine-quality natural fiber cloth. Synthetics are generally blended with the natural fibers for a few very worthy causes—to overcome a definite drawback to the natural fiber, to lower costs, or to make for easy care. They can make linen more crease-resistant, make silk machine-washable, and so on. The benefits and drawbacks of natural/synthetic blends tally in accordance to the percentage of the synthetic added. In simple terms, the higher the percentage of man-made fibers, the more synthetic properties the finished cloth will have. So while a fifty/fifty wool/acrylic blend might be easier to maintain, it might not breathe as well or feel as good next to the skin as pure wool. My main warning concerning blends and all-synthetic fabrics is simply not to be enticed by convenience at the expense of the look and feel.

The only man-made fiber I personally ever

Raw silk and silk shantung are best for suits, slacks and jackets.

feel comfortable wearing is rayon. It's a cool fabric that seems to me to breathe as well as natural fibers and has none of the clamminess that I associate with other synthetics. The probable reason for this is that, although rayon is classified as a man-made fiber, it is technically not a true synthetic because its source is natural (cellulose derived from cotton linters and wood pulp) rather than chemical.

The granddaddy of man-made fibers, rayon was first made in Paris in 1889 to resemble silk and was actually called artificial silk for many years. Today it not only imitates silk but also simulates various textures of wool, linen, and cotton. Good rayons have a quality look and feel, are comparatively inexpensive, and are easy to maintain. If you are looking for an alternative to the natural fibers, I think rayon heads the list.

In the final analysis, whether considering man-made fibers or blends or natural cloth, the bottom line is how a fabric looks and feels. The fiber content will give you clues as to a fabric's durability, comfort, maintenance, suitability, and general attractiveness. But it will not guarantee a quality look. Due to variations of yarn construction, weaving processes, and finishes, even the age-old reliable natural fibers produce both good and bad grades of cloth.

Let's consider the natural fibers individually and discuss some of the winning fabrics they produce—the ones that are best suited for our purposes and the ones that always look rich.

Silk

Silk charmeuse and silk crepe de chine lend themselves to exquisite draping.

SILK HAS ALWAYS been considered the fabric of royalty and aristocracy, from as far back as 1725 B.C., when silk culture, sponsored by the wife of the emperor, was begun in China, to the present day, when the production and glories of the luxurious silk that made up Lady Di's (the Princess of Wales, that is) wedding dress received special media attention.

Silk is simply the most elegant-looking fabric in the world. It exudes a quiet, understated opulence. Its natural, lustrous texture says rich—quietly.

A few very special, select silk garments are an indispensable part of a classically chic wardrobe. Silks are sophisticated and feminine without being frilly, which makes them perfectly suited for business situations where you want to have a definite but unintimidating aura of success. They are life savers when you don't know just how dressy a certain occasion will be. You'd be hard pressed to look either overdressed or underdressed in a simple, elegant silk shirtwaist or a wonderful silk blouse and a great pair of slacks. In short, silk is extremely versatile—perfect for day or evening, almost any occasion and every season, except perhaps the dead heat of summer.

Silk can be made into a vast variety of fabrics and textures, from the sheerest chiffon and organza to the most luxurious brocades and velvets, all wonderful in their own ways. For our plan, however, certain silks are more practical than others. Our best bets are crepe de chine and charmeuse, which are ideal for blouses and dresses, and raw silk and shantung, which have a stiffer, nubby feel and are great for suits, jackets, and slacks.

The best-designed silk blouses and dresses take advantage of the exquisite drape that silk allows and are made from a heavy-to-medium weight silk. The fabric should have a good substantial feel to it and not be too thin or flimsy. A label that reads "pure silk" means that no metallic salts have been added to increase the weight and give it a heavier "hand," but it doesn't indicate the actual weight of the cloth. The best way to train your eye and touch to discern between the "lightweights" and the "heavyweights" is by comparison. Take a look at some of the top designer silks, most of which are of excellent quality and the perfect weight. Then have a look at a few "special bargain" thirty-dollar blouses. You'll find yourself a very discerning customer in no time.

Wool

THERE IS no substitute for good wool. The comfort and aristocratic look of fine cashmeres, flannels, tweeds, camel's hair, and gabardine—to name just a few of the most elegant fabrics—simply cannot be duplicated. Quality wools are not cheap, but they are worth every penny. They hold up especially well and will always be thoroughly fashionable.

The quality of wool depends on a multitude of factors, ranging from the home territory of the sheep (or goat in the case of cashmere and camel in the case of camel's hair) and the care the animal gets to the time and skill applied to the numerous and intricate processes involved in turning the fiber into cloth. Needless to say, none of these factors is mentioned on the label. Labels here, as with all fabric, are merely a guarantee as to the content. Once again you are left to rely on your visual and tactile senses.

Essentially, what you are looking for in quality wools is softness, a fine, close, even weave, a springy warm feel, and a pleasingly substantial weight. Even a high-quality specialty fabric like cashmere loses its class if the cloth is thin and loosely woven.

Wool textures can introduce subtle patterns in a most sophisticated way.

Cotton

ALL CONSIDERED, cotton is a real bargain among textiles. You can't beat it for comfort and practicality in the hot summer months. It has a wonderful feel, is durable and inexpensive to maintain, and, generally speaking, it is the least costly of the natural fibers.

The quality of cotton cloth is primarily dependent on the species of cotton from which it is derived. While it is interesting to note that those varieties with the longest and finest fibers produce the best fabrics, you actually need very little of this technical knowledge to be able to spot top-grade cotton fabrics. In short, the finer the cotton the better the quality *and* the richer the look.

No one could question the fact that a superb, finely woven, polished Egyptian cotton looks and feels 100 percent more elegant than the best chambray or denim. Even with a fabric like corduroy, the finer the wale the richer the look. Gauzy Indian cottons, while admittedly cool and practical, never look especially classy. Best to limit them to very casual and weekend wear.

Linen

GOOD LINEN is another terrific summer fabric. It is cool, durable, soil-resistant, washable, has a look of affluence, and, as an extra bonus, it actually improves with age. Although I am a true linen fan and fully appreciate its winning qualities, I don't consider it as indispensable for our purposes as the other natural fibers. You could easily build a very chic wardrobe with silk, wool and cotton alone.

The Irish still produce the best quality linens, and because of the high cost of production and manufacturing, fine Irish linen is expensive. Another consideration is that linen fiber is not elastic and therefore is quick to wrinkle even when treated for crease resistance. A linen dress worn through an entire working day would not be terribly fresh-looking by evening. A silk crepe dress would. A linen jacket, on the other hand, that could be worn on and off during the day would most likely be in fine shape for an early spring or summer dinner. And because linen doesn't drape well, it is much better suited to jackets, slacks and skirts, anyway. Also, since it doesn't take especially well to dyes, your best bet is to stick to natural linen, which runs in the beige family, or to linen that is bleached a pure, snowy white.

Leathers

IN SUMMING UP this fabric discussion I should say a few words about leathers. Very soft, pliable, fine suedes, calf, pigskin, and kid can be quite elegant in a classic, sporty way. These will undoubtedly prove to be quite expensive. Hard, stiff, cheap leathers look just that. They are lowbrow and unacceptable. Once again the last word is that if you can't afford the best leathers, forget them altogether.

If you do allow yourself the luxury of fine leather garments, remember that maintenance cost is high as well. It could cost as much as $30 to clean a simple pair of suede slacks. Better then to go for a darker shade that doesn't show dirt easily.

3

THE
PLAN:
THEORY
INTO
PRACTICE

The Plan

When you're working with a tight budget, a memorable, one-time appearance dress like this wouldn't be a true bargain—even if it were marked down twice.

AND NOW for the final stage of our plan: actually pulling together the consummate wardrobe. In theory it's an easy task. But practically, even with our new knowledge, it will still take some solid planning, concentrated time, and a relatively substantial initial investment. Not surprisingly, the less money you have to devote to the cause, the more thought and shopping time is required.

There is no getting around the fact that Dressing Rich calls for some up-front expenditures on classic clothes and accessories. You need a few major investment pieces to serve as the core of your new wardrobe, to upgrade moderately priced pieces, and to add new life to the items you already have in your wardrobe that will be quite usable with a little help. Once you've made your initial investment, however, your greatest expense will be behind you. Clothes bills will never again be as high. They will decrease each year as you simply make a few new additions each season to your solid foundation.

One more point I must make—even at the risk of being repetitive—is the matter of amortization. The real cost of clothing or an accessory is not simply the amount marked on the price tag. You also have to consider the wear you get from it, the self-confidence and elegance it affords you, and how much you enjoy wearing it. That's why you have to watch so-called bargains. A $200 dress that looks smashing, is comfortable, and that you can wear frequently and for many years is many times more a bargain than a $30 sale dress that you only wear once. That's not to say that you should ignore the sales. When you know exactly what you want and need, sales can be a boon—especially those at the seasons' ends. The point is not to buy things simply because they are on sale, no matter how great the temptation, but because you need it and luckily it's on sale.

Before we get into the specifics of formulating a new wardrobe, let's talk briefly about the clothing you already own, thrift-shop buys on vintage classics, and the viability of home sewing.

"Old" Clothes

WE WOULD BE at cross purposes to let our enthusiasm for creating a new and elegant wardrobe either divert our attention from the potential chic of some of the garments in our current wardrobe, or cause us to overlook the possibility of long-forgotten treasures hidden away in the back recesses of our closets or crated and stored in Mom's attic.

Before you activate your new wardrobe plan, it is a good idea to go through every last stitch of clothing you already own—leaving no drawers unturned—and try to assess the value and serviceability of each item. It is highly probable that you own some clothes that can be successfully integrated, as is, into your new wardrobe and others that can be altered, restyled, reaccessorized and generally renovated to accommodate your new image.

The probability, of course, is even higher that during your thorough investigation you will come across other old clothes that have simply outlived their usefulness. These

Items like these have outlived their usefulness and simply have to go.

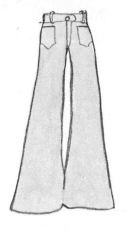

should be immediately donated to your favorite charitable organization. There is no sense in keeping them around and deluding yourself that you have a full working wardrobe when in fact none of it is wearable.

What to throw away and what to keep—that is the question. Quality must be the deciding factor. Old polyester pajama pants, snug little nylon blouses with cute pink floral motifs, adorable puffy-sleeved baby blue empire-style dresses, satin mini-skirts, and on and on, have no place in an elegant wardrobe. Toss them out. Other "oldies but goodies" like a hearty old cashmere sweater, a four-year-old charcoal gray flannel straight skirt, Mom's wonderful old tweed coat, a seasoned pair of chamois slacks, or perhaps an ancient mink stole, for instance, are viable candidates for recycling. Let's not forget that old, quality clothes have "Old Guard chic" potential.

You might find some irreplaceable "oldies" that are rather démodé at the moment and cannot be restyled to capture a modern look, since a basic silhouette is often more difficult to modify than collars, sleeves, lapels, and other detailing. Mom's old tweed coat might possibly fall into this category. This type of old, quality fashion can be stored away for timely return appearances. Who knows? That coat might be terribly *au courant* in five years.

Accessories go by the same rules. If it was not a quality treasure when it first came into your life, toss it. Old platform shoes, vinyl-trimmed handbags, flimsy leather belts and chipped costume jewelry no longer belong in your wardrobe or even your storage cartons. Fine alligator belts, good quality loafers, or fine Shetland sweaters might have rerun possibilities and should be considered for storing.

The point is to get everything out of your closet that doesn't complement your new image. Unloading friendly old clothes may prove to be somewhat traumatic, for it seems the older the clothes the more sentimental attachment is involved. But be brave and put sentiment aside. It is actually quite a comfortable feeling to look in your closet and see only fine, wearable clothing—even if that closet is only half full.

By the way, if you are storing clothes, it is a good idea to label each box with its exact contents. There are few things more annoying than searching through the deep, dark recesses of a closet or attic while muttering, "I know it's in here somewhere." You can never go wrong with a little organization.

Quality oldies have recycle potential. Incorporate them in your new wardrobe or store them for future use.

Thrift Shops

IF YOU HAVE THE TIME, a good eye, and a spirit of adventure, you can find some very reasonably priced old classic treasures at thrift shops, especially those that are run by high society's pet charities. Patience and perseverance are also handy virtues to have when going the thrift-store route. It usually takes a careful sifting through racks and racks of shabby and otherwise mediocre clothing to find one wonderful buried treasure. Of course, timing helps. Some days there is absolutely nothing to be found. Other days will produce a bonanza.

I must admit that I am not one of the all-time-great thrift-store shoppers. Since shopping was a good part of my job for so long, I still subconsciously think of it more as work than pleasure. To be a successful thrift-store shopper you must above all enjoy the thrill of the hunt as well as the kill. I do have a few thrift-shop aficionado friends who thoroughly enjoy the pursuit and have come up with bargains that are incredible enough to make even a recalcitrant shopper like myself want to visit local shops every now and again. Here are some of their finds:

- Off-white long silk bathrobe—looks almost new: $15 (Reminiscent of a swishy boudoir scene in a '40s movie—Claudette Colbert, perhaps. No alterations needed; $4 for cleaning.)
- Navy blue cashmere coat in mint condition: $15 (plus $100 to have it tailored for a perfect fit)
- Harris tweed hacking jacket: $10 (plus another $50 to have it relined. Tailors

commented: "You just can't find this quality tweed anymore.")

- Classic black gabardine straight skirt with a black kick pleat, Yves Saint Laurent label, fully lined: $5
- Black cashmere cape: $50
- English paisley shawl, superb fabric: $5
- Burgundy alligator belt: $3
- Long, full, fringed light-beige scarf of soft and heavy silk: $8 (plus $4 for cleaning)

And the list goes on and on—great beaded and alligator handbags, silk pocket squares, hand-knit sweaters, ascots, tortoiseshell hair combs, cuff links, wonderfully classic old paste jewelry . . .

As I said, it takes luck and perseverance to find items like these, and they will often need to be altered or restyled to look great once again. But when you consider the quality of material and workmanship you're getting at cut-rate prices, they are quite marvelous bargains.

Auctions

CLOTHING AUCTIONS are a relatively new phenomenon. Good deals can assuredly be had, but since you'd be bidding against fashion experts—both professional collectors and very savvy enthusiasts—you really have to know your stuff to come out a winner. Sotheby Parke Bernet and Christie's hold clothing and accessory auctions at least twice a year in New York. Sotheby's also auctions clothing at their Los Angeles branch.

The price and vintage of auction pieces span a wide range. Some antique items are

pure collectables and would hardly be much of a contribution to a modern-day wardrobe, such as brocade or taffeta visiting costumes circa 1870. More recent items, however, have potential, like crepe or beaded evening dresses and jackets from the 1920s or '30s, which might range from $50 to $200. Beaded pocketbooks also might go for $50 to $200. Ensembles by fifties and sixties designers, including Mainboucher, Adrian, Balenciaga, Chanel, and others can cost anywhere from $60 to $700. And there was one spectacular Trigère black cashmere cape, circa 1960, at SPB a few seasons ago that listed for $100 to $150 that I found irresistible.

These auctions are often very educational as well as a lot of fun. They are definitely a worthwhile experience even if you end up buying nothing. If you are not in the New York or Los Angeles vicinity you can write to the subscription departments of both Christie's and Sotheby Parke Bernet and request the clothing collectables catalogue. It is possible to bid by mail, but it is always better to see the pieces ahead of time. It's more exciting that way.

Sotheby Parke Bernet
980 Madison Avenue
New York, NY 10021

Christie's Catalogue Subscription
141 East 25th Street
New York, NY 10010

Home Sewing

IT WOULD BE a grave oversight not to mention home sewing as a very viable possibility in the Dressing Rich scheme of things. The amount of money that can be saved by creating your own fashions can be enormous. Some designer skirts, for instance, that cost as much as $100 in the stores could easily be turned out at home for under $20. That's more than a 75 percent saving.

This considered, you would think that home sewing would be extremely popular today when everyone is feeling the economic crunch to some degree, but many women seem to feel that it requires too much time and too great an expertise. When I conducted a rather informal poll, the most common comments I heard were, "Are you kidding? I can't even sew a straight line," and "I don't even have time to think, much less drag out and dust off the sewing machine." Neither of these well-taken points is necessarily valid.

First of all, you don't have to be a bona

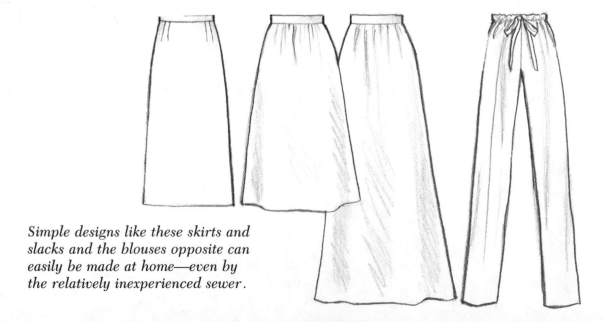

Simple designs like these skirts and slacks and the blouses opposite can easily be made at home—even by the relatively inexperienced sewer.

fide *haute couture* seamstress to whip up a few basic, simple styles—like a straight or dirndl skirt, for instance. And let's not forget that simplicity is one of the keys to looking rich. Needless to say, it would totally defeat our purpose if the clothes we quickly whip up *look* homemade, but that will rarely happen if you stay within the limitations of your skill. If you are a beginner, steer clear of intricate designs. If you stick to easy styles—and there are many that require no more than a few well-placed seams—you can produce some very professional-looking, classy pieces of merchandise.

Secondly, once you have invested relatively little time in practice, you'll find that you can turn out a fine, easy-to-sew garment in no time at all, and that you can do it while watching television or listening to your favorite symphony. Also remember that it takes a great deal of time to find exactly what you want in the stores. Shopping time can actually exceed sewing time.

Another big plus to home sewing is that it provides a tremendous freedom of fabric choice. When you buy ready-to-wear clothes you have a relatively limited material choice within the context of a particular design, which is why shopping is often so time-consuming. You might find a garment with the perfect design and fit, but in the wrong fabric, texture, or color. When you make your own clothes, you pick the design *and* the material that will suit your needs.

Clever use of materials can turn simple patterns into very sophisticated ensembles. Contrasting fabrics is a favorite trick of some top designers. Gianfranco Ferre, for example, created a quite elegant evening costume last season when he combined a loose tunic top of luxurious beige silk shot with a gold design with a pair of simple, fresh, white cotton pants.

The pattern companies produce designs suitable to every level of sewing proficiency, from novice to expert. "Very Easy" patterns are created for "the contemporary woman who has a lot of fashion savvy and little time for sewing." These patterns combine high fashion styling with very easy construction techniques and are ideal for beginners. For the skilled sewer there are *haute couture* patterns from many top American and European designers: Yves Saint Laurent, Givenchy, Karl Lagerfeld, Valentino, Bill Blass, Oscar de la Renta, and Calvin Klein, to name a few.

If you are interested in giving sewing a whirl but don't know where to start, you can buy one of the introductory sewing books put out by some of the pattern companies. For the most part, they are easy to understand and afford a fairly thorough look at what you would need to know in order to start.

The Foundation

THE Dressing Rich wardrobe plan is largely based on one easy, major premise:
> *At least one part of any outfit you wear must be of top quality, look unquestionably expensive, and be in subtle and exquisite taste.*

The trick, of course, is to use one or two "unquestionable" pieces of a particular outfit to establish rank, lend credibility, and upgrade the rest of the ensemble—which can be pretty moderately priced as long as it is understated, simple and tasteful.

These "upgrading" items are the investment buys that I mentioned earlier. They are the versatile and select pieces with a universal status look, such as a Harris tweed jacket, cashmere sweater, alligator handbag, gold Rolex watch, simple antique gold necklace, a pair of fine leather pumps, and so on. If you stick with the prescribed color and design plan, you'll find that a few wise investments like these will take you a long way—and in first-class seats.

Your first major investments should be clothes and accessories whose quality cannot be easily duplicated and that you would wear most often. The latter, of course, depends upon your individual demands. A pair of classic, impeccably cut gray flannel trousers might be a wise first investment choice for me, but would be low on the priority list of a career woman who worked in a conservative office where women's slacks are discouraged.

Shoes and handbags are wise first investments, no matter what your lifestyle. Cheap imitations here stand out like a sore thumb, while the best of the lot will add a dash of elegance to any outfit. Jackets, coats, and the perennial, versatile "little black dress" are other front-runners for early investment. While a $175 elegant silk charmeuse blouse (like the one on the dust

A lightweight blue blazer works as well with a tailored dress as with slacks.

jacket) or a $1,500 string of pearls would in the long run prove to be worthwhile investments, their general look can be duplicated for much less money—and they wouldn't look elegant at all if worn with a cheap bag and shoes. A simple, reasonably priced blouse and skirt with a string of good imitation pearls could, on the other hand, appear quite rich if worn with exquisite shoes and bag, and topped with a wonderful jacket.

Since I have no way of knowing the contents of your present wardrobe or your particular climate, let's approach the wardrobe plan from scratch—as if you have an empty closet and live in a four-season climate. This general plan is designed to suit most "average" lifestyles and is the minimum framework on which to build. If your demands are exceptional—say, you run around a recording studio all day or have to attend biweekly black-tie benefits—you will obviously have to alter the plan a bit to suit. Add or subtract according to your individual situation.

The best way to structure your framework is to adapt the major part of your wardrobe to the two extreme seasons, summer and winter. With minor additions, spring and fall will take care of themselves, with some of your winter clothes covering the cool fall and spring days and the summer clothing standing in for warm spring and autumn days. This crossover plan is especially practical in these days of controlled indoor climates. Even in the dead of summer you'll often need a sweater or jacket to ward off the chills of air conditioning.

While I'm not an ardent suit advocate, I am a hearty supporter of separates. When it comes to practicality, convenience, and flexibility of use, suits come out a first-place winner. By alternating jackets, wearing cardigans, and sporting blouses in different styles and color, you'll find a few suits will go a long way, looking elegant all the while.

The following is what I consider an excellent skeletal wardrobe. Needless to say, all these pieces should be of superior quality and will be your long-term investment pieces.

Summer Framework

- *Lightweight wool navy blazer (or cardigan-style jacket)*—This handy little classic will look great in any season. It can be worn over cool tailored dresses and with skirts and slacks. In the summer it is especially good with white linen. The navy and white combination has a very affluent look about it. Great for yachting, too.
- *One suit in a beige tone*—Of either linen, a linenlike fabric, or raw silk. The style should be one that is easily dressed up or down with accessories. The skirt should be a straight classic. It can go to work, a wedding, or a social dinner. Jacket and skirt can be worn separately. Two such suits would be ideal, the second in a dark tone. But they are expensive, and you can always add the other next year.
- *One off-white jacket*—Cool fabric—linen, silk, or cotton. The choice of style should

A well-designed silk blouse can be worn in a variety of ways.

complement your personality, either casual or tailored.

- *One "little black dress" in silk*—If black is unflattering to you, choose another of the dark neutrals. This fashion staple can literally go anywhere in any season. It should be of timeless design and incredibly well made. And if this "little black dress" is actually a skirt and blouse ensemble designed to look like a dress, you have even more options.
- *One simple shirtwaist dress*—This can be either a solid or a print, but if it's the latter it must be a subtle one on a dark background (red on navy, for instance). If you're more of a "beige person," a taupe background might be more to your liking. In this specific category you could easily substitute a separates ensemble with a dresslike appearance.
- *Two fine silk blouses*—One light, one dark. They should be of the finest design and quality. Should go beautifully with the suits but should be able to stand on their own, too. Good back detail, moderately sized collars. A yoke with exquisite draping would be an excellent choice for full-bosomed women.
- *Two pairs of classic, straight trousers*—One off-white, one black, in raw silk. These can be dressed up with a silk blouse or down with a cotton one.
- *Two great belts*—One light, one dark. Can be varying shades of your light and dark neutrals. Should be of a flattering width to go with everything.
- *One cashmere cardigan*—In your favorite

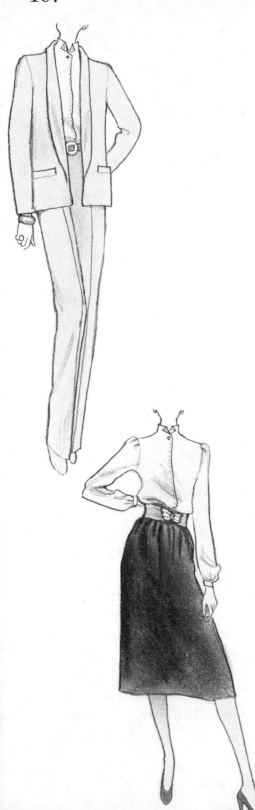

secondary color (slate blue would be a good choice). Another seasonless staple. Casually worn over the shoulders, it can create another look for the dress or blouse beneath.

- *Two pairs of shoes*—One light (not white!), one dark. These must be quality all the way. If cost is prohibitive, buy the dark first, add the light when you can afford it. A medium-heel, classic pump would be the most practical because you could easily wear it in any season. An elegant sandal would also be suitable for summer. It's best to stick to calf and forgo patent leather.
- *Two handbags*—Neutrals: one light, one dark. Again, they must be of superior quality and will probably be expensive. They should last for years. Not too large, but roomy enough to be practical. (And again, go for the dark first if you can only afford one now.)

These items constitute the framework of your investment wardrobe for summer (and part of fall and spring) and should see you through many years. The additions can be less expensive and less classic, since you won't be demanding the same longevity of them. The quantity of supplements is up to you and your budget. But you should add the following minimum to complete your summer wardrobe—and they can be in a moderate price range (anywhere from $30 to $70).

A second fine silk blouse can be worn as effectively with an off-white linen jacket and slacks as with the skirt from the dark suit opposite.

MODERATELY PRICED ADDITIONS

- *Two skirts*—One light, one dark, in cool summer fabrics. The styles don't have to be as classic as your suit skirt, but they ought to flatter your figure as nicely. A full off-white or white skirt that you could wear with a cotton T-shirt might be a fun extra.
- *One pair of khaki slacks*
- *A lightweight, fine cotton, all-around dress*—In a flattering shade that will look casually elegant with flat sandals or espadrilles.
- *Two fine cotton blouses*—Your choice of style and color.

The rest is completely individual. Add as many T-shirts, little cotton skirts, shorts, slacks, canvas shoes, sandals, or fun straw accessories as you see fit.

Winter Framework

BEFORE WE get into the winter framework, we need a quick word about one of your most important purchases—your winter coat. The material basically comes down to a choice between fur, wool, and recently, down.

Although I love down for its warmth and light weight, it is, unfortunately, not a particularly rich or elegant look. You can "get by" with a down coat during the day—especially with sporty clothes—but you'd be hard-put to make it look really chic for any kind of evening wear. Down is not a great choice for your only coat, but it makes a super second coat.

Fur can look gloriously elegant—certainly nothing looks richer than a full, luxurious, dark mink coat. But who can afford that? Mink and other fine furs are at a premium these days. As far as I'm concerned, if you can't afford the very best, it's better to do without. Inexpensive, so-called "fun furs," are antithetical to Dressing Rich.

Wool coats don't have to be as boring as Richard Nixon made them sound in his memorable Checkers Speech ("My wife, Pat, doesn't wear mink. She wears a respectable,

The classic tie coat

The smock coat

Republican cloth coat. And I always tell her she'd look good in anything.") Somehow it just doesn't sound like Dick really appreciates how chic wool can be.

Plain wool, cashmere, camel's hair, and tweed make splendid-looking coats. Tweed is especially handsome. If you can afford only one coat, wool is your best choice. It will be perfectly elegant and suitable for most occasions, save a coronation or a very fancy ball, in which case you won't need a coat anyway thanks to your limousine.

Your choice of style and color deserves some careful consideration, since your coat will be your constant companion for an entire season and hopefully for many years. It should be flattering, practical, chic, and relatively easy to maintain. Again, as with all investment buys, the lines should be simple and refined, the fabric of excellent quality, and the workmanship impeccable (or, at least as impeccable as one can find these days). Superfluous detailing—nonfunctional seams and insets or purely decorative buttons—should be avoided. The cut and fit are very important. Your coat should be roomy enough to wear a lightweight jacket beneath and fitted enough to provide an attractive silhouette.

It's a good idea to stick to our color plan when deciding on color. Any of the rich neutrals would be fine. The fact that the lighter colors show dirt more readily and have to be cleaned more often should be a concern. Bright colors—especially red—can be quite attractive and cheery on a somber

The full-swing, raglan-sleeve classic

winter day, but a dark neutral would probably (though not necessarily) be better for evening. I have seen incredible red coats and capes that would be the height of chic in any situation.

Creative touches with fur can turn a simple cloth coat into a vision of real old-time

Fur trimming can add new life and chic to a simple, old coat.

elegance. A detachable mink collar and cuffs, for instance, could make a gray flannel coat as dressy for night as it is sporty for day. This is an especially good tactic if you have any old fur stoles tucked away in your closet that are still in decent shape. (Check your relatives' closets, too!) Good-quality old minks can be made into raincoat linings, which can have an extremely rich look.

Now on to the recommended winter wardrobe framework.

- *Winter coat*—Oatmeal-fleck or black-and-white tweed would be excellent choices, as would gray flannel or black or navy cashmere.
- *One heavy wool tweed suit*—The skirt should be a straight classic. The jacket should be tailored and the style flexible enough to wear as a fall jacket.
- *One gray flannel suit*—Classic style. It can also be a more flattering dark neutral if desired.
- *One elegant black suit*—Or jacket and skirt separates with a suitlike appearance. The jacket can be loose yet sophisticated, and the skirt should be simple and easy. Wool gabardine or wool crepe would be good choices.
- *One cashmere turtleneck sweater*—The color is your choice. You can also choose a V-neck if it is a better style for you.
- *One black cashmere tunic-style sweater*

By simply interchanging pieces of your compact winter wardrobe . . .

- *One cashmere sweater jacket*—Beige, gray, or black, or any color other than that of your summer cardigan, of course—both are seasonless. Black would be ideal since it could be worn for slightly dressy evening affairs.

. . . you can achieve a variety of looks.

- *One good wool pullover*—In your choice of color. This can be worn over shirts or with scarves, and with or without a jacket.
- *Charcoal gray flannel slacks*—If these don't look good on you, you could choose a neutral-colored skirt in a sporty style.
- *Black tailored wool slacks*

- *One cashmere sweater dress*—Black, gray, beige, or any of the rich neutrals. It may even work in one of the secondary colors like deep plum. This is a great all-around garment that can be dressed up or down.
- *One pair of extra-special, fine calfskin boots*—Dark neutral color, medium untrendy heel and style.
- *One pair of "English walking shoes"*
- *Good-looking foul weather boots*
- *One pair of classic pumps*—These can be a crossover from your summer wardrobe if you can't afford a second pair.

MODERATELY PRICED ADDITIONS

- *One tweed skirt*—A style flattering to your figure.
- *Two cotton or wool flannel shirts*—These are to wear with sweaters. They should be of colors complementary both to your foundation pieces and to you.
- *Two extra sweaters*—In your choice of color, and in any classic style, such as V-neck.

Evening Looks

WITHIN THE GENERAL frameworks above, you'll find yourself well set for almost any possible situation with the exception of bona fide black-tie affairs. Since the chances are the occasion will arise when you will need some sort of real formal attire—to attend the Oscars, gala performances, posh benefits, or art exhibit openings—it's a good idea to be somewhat prepared in order to avoid last-minute panic, which can cause ulcers, wrinkles, and general insanity.

The main thing here is not to be set back or intimidated by the mere mention of "black tie" or the grandiosity of the event. You don't need a lot of ruffles, sequins, yard-wide taffeta skirts, or elaborate dresses for even the biggest of evenings. Simplicity still reigns supreme. The feeling of luxury and opulence that is called for at formal gatherings can be more elegantly achieved through wise choice of fabric, color, and simple, understated design than with frills and feathers.

Think fabric first. Silks, satins, panne velvet, lace, subtle metallic prints in black with gold or the like will immediately set a dressy tone.

Black again is always a winning color choice. It provides a sleek evening silhouette, always looks elegant, can easily accommodate a switch of accessories to make for new and different looks, and allows you to make double use of some of your black winter wardrobe basics. A pair of wool crepe slacks, for instance, can look sporty in the day with a Harris tweed blazer and dressy at night with a gold-flecked blouse and metallic belt. The most practical design approach is to build the total look with pieces that are simple in shape but luxurious in texture. A skirt that is soft, narrow-falling and ankle long, for instance, could be worn with a beautiful, soft tunic top, a spectacular blouse with dolman or pleated sleeves, or even a camisole and small quilted jacket. The tops could also be worn with a soft, silk "pajama" pant for a completely different silhouette. Separates, even in evening wear, are more versatile than a dress or gown that has only one look. When money is an issue, versatility is a key word.

Black-tie gala

Whenever you're in the stores, keep your eyes open for pieces with "formal potential." End-of-summer sales are an especially good time since they have to move out the silks and satins to make room for tweeds and flannels. At the end of last summer I found a terrific pair of light beige silk charmeuse straight pajama pants reduced from $250 to $70. Now all I need is the opportunity to wear them. But as I said, it's always best to be prepared when the invitation arrives.

We've sketched some great evening looks, both formal and casually dressy, to show you the kind of mileage you can get out of a few basic black dressy separates, and to give you an idea of the varied and elegant looks you can create with a few simple additions. And these are just a few examples of the endless combinations possible.

Our basic pieces are a long silk-velvet skirt, with an impeccable drape, neither too full nor too narrow; a simple, easy, street-length silk skirt; easy-falling silk charmeuse pajama pants; a silk camisole. Remember, too, that you already have a black cashmere tunic, classic black slacks, and a cashmere "smoking jacket" style sweater in your winter wardrobe that can easily be worn in the evening.

The basics I suggest here will never be out of fashion. They will provide a multitude of looks year after year; they are true investment items. You will have to buy a new blouse, new belt, and various other accessories from time to time to give these basics new life and a current look. But the cost will always be considerably less than

buying a completely new outfit every year. And the new pieces can always be used to perk up your daytime wardrobe as well.

1. *For a dinner with friends or entertaining at home:* Black cashmere sweater tunic, black slacks from the winter wardrobe. For interest and dash add a gold belt and gold cuff bracelet . . . or wear it unbelted and add gold chains.

2. *For a holiday evening:* Wear the tunic tucked in and simply substitute your long velvet skirt for the wool slacks. Or wear the long skirt with a silk charmeuse T-shirt type blouse or a creamy satin blouse with lace detail. You could also wear a translucent gold chiffon blouse with dolman sleeves and a softly draped bow at the neck.

3. *For a black-tie gala:* Pair your faithful velvet skirt with a simple, bare-shouldered velvet halter top. Add some simple rhinestone jewelry (or diamonds, if you have them) and a simple, elegant belt. The outfit will give the impression of a unique evening gown, and you will appear to be as expensively clad as the titled gentry around you.

4. *For a casually formal artsy event:* Don your black slacks, a simple, jewel-neck, white silk shirt, your cashmere sweater-jacket, a great belt or necklace. Push up your sleeves for that unstudied look and you're all set.

5. *For that special out-on-the-town evening:* The black silk slacks paired with an excellent silver- and black-sequined camisole or a gold-sequined, long-sleeved, boat-neck

blouse will immediately create a lasting impression. If it's a bit chilly, your cashmere sweater-jacket will keep you warm in style.

Accessories

ACCESSORIES play an important role in our plan. They can help you get maximum mileage from a small, compact wardrobe, provide new life for old classics, and can make a $40 outfit look like it cost $200. Let's briefly discuss each specific accessory category, starting with the most basic: shoes.

Shoes

SHOES HAVE BEEN CALLED "the perfect barometer of elegance," and I couldn't agree more. As I mentioned before, cheap shoes shine like a beacon and could easily destroy all that we've worked so diligently for. This doesn't mean that shoes have to cost a fortune. They should simply be the classiest of their classes: pumps, casual sandals, espadrilles, loafers, tennis and running shoes, boots, and the rest.

It is not just fine quality materials that make a shoe "classy." It is equally important that it look good on your foot, compliment your leg, work well proportionately in terms of your entire body and outfit, and, of course, be comfortable. If a shoe meets all these qualifications it is a winner—and usually expensive. It's hard to find a good pair of everyday shoes for less than $75, and they are

Low-cut shallow pump

Classic slingback

Classic Chanel slingback

THE BEST BETS

generally more. Remember, though, that it's not just top quality materials and workmanship you are paying for (which sometimes looks minimal, especially in the case of an elegant evening sandal made with only a few strips of leather and a sole), but the design as well. Well-designed shoes are most often high-priced but are worth the money for the positive effect they have on the proportion and balance of your overall look.

A low-cut, shallow pump or a low-cut slingback with a medium-height, narrowish heel are very flattering designs for most women, and are best bets for an everyday shoe. A low-cut, shallow shoe interferes very little with the line of the leg and gives it a long, slim look. Even Gucci-type walking shoes look more elegant when the tongue or flap on top of the shoe is cut low and allows more of the instep to show. Styles with ankle straps, on the other hand, are generally unflattering. And so, to a lesser degree, are any shoes with T-straps and straps across the instep. They interrupt the line of the leg and make it appear shorter. In general, the less shoe there is, the better the leg will look.

For dressy evening occasions a simple, elegant, slingback-type strappy sandal will at most always look good. The heel can be slightly higher if you like—but not at the expense of a graceful stride. Some high-heeled shoes look wonderful in the store but are impossible to walk in. Don't be tempted by the look alone. Nothing can be more inelegant than an awkward, tottering gait.

Trendy and faddish shoes go by the same

The espadrille

Classic tassel loafer

English walking shoe

rules we've established for ultra-voguish clothes: they should usually be avoided. Following trends is simply not rich, in any case. An exception here is flat-soled shoes that have made a fashionable comeback. Moccasins, modified ballet slippers, flat boots and sandals have been around forever and are classics in that respect. The problem is that not everybody looks good in them (and I have to include myself). You have to be rather tall—five feet, seven inches or more—or be very evenly proportioned to wear flat shoes successfully. Most women need a slight heel to look their best. If you opt for a flat shoe, make sure it is perfectly suited to you. Don't wear them just because they are "in."

Certainly, it is important to remember that all accessories—and especially shoes—follow the current fashion trends quite closely. They take their cues from shoulder widths, hemlines, and the general fashion theme. Accessories complete the silhouette. If you wear an "accessory of the moment," like flat shoes, you must take extra care that they are perfectly in tune with the rest of your ensemble.

The best bet for your first investment shoe is a well-cut (and low-cut) classic pump made of the finest calfskin. Since fine leather pumps are perfect for any season and are adaptable to any time of the day, they would prove a most flexible choice. Calf with suede or patent trimming, or suede pumps can be very handsome, but since they are less versatile, they are a better selection as a second or third pair. The Chanel two-toned

123

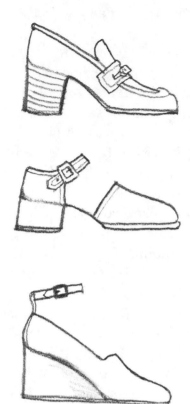

THE REAL RISKS

slingback is another classic that always looks smart and is wonderfully comfortable—a great choice for your second pair of shoes.

Color, of course, should be neutral, a tone that complements your foundation wardrobe. Black or a shade of brown would be logical and ideal for the first pair. Brightly colored shoes (and bags), while they can be marvelously fun, are impractical for our purposes and rarely look rich. Exceptions here are only among casual shoes, for vacation wear, like a red or a lavender sandal, which can be very amusing. Aside from black and beige, natural luggage, gray, and taupe are exceptionally chic in leather accessories.

White shoes tend to look a bit provincial on city streets, and they also tend to make the foot appear a bit large. Bone color would, in most cases, be a better choice if you'd like a lighter tone.

Shoes should complement and add elegance to an outfit, never make a statement in and of themselves. When your shoes and handbag are the best and your clothes well chosen, no one would think to question the legitimacy of your tasteful "expensive" jewelry or the "high cost" of your becoming ensemble.

Say, for instance, that you are wearing a taupe wool skirt, a beige silk blouse, and a taupe cashmere sweater. You have added a pearl necklace, pearl earrings set in gold, a gold watch, a simple gold band ring, and a marvelous pair of pumps with a matchless handbag. Who would suspect that the blouse and skirt were moderately priced, the cardigan three years old, the pearls imitation, and the jewelry only gold-plated? It would occur to no one, and that's a guarantee.

Boots

THERE IS A TIME and a place for boots. They are especially practical outdoors on cold and blustery days, can look quite smart with fall and winter coats, and are a natural in the country. Indoors, however, they rarely look smart unless they are worn with slacks or are an integral part of your outfit. The problem again is proportion. When you wear skirts or dresses, boots add an extra dimension to your legs and require the bulk of a coat, jacket, or at least a layered "big top" look to create a pleasing balance. On the street, of course, this is not a problem, but once you move out of the natural environment and into heated rooms your outer layers (and excess bulk) come off, the proportion shifts, and boots suddenly seem too heavy for your outfit. If you wear boots and plan to be inside most of the day it's a good idea to bring along a pair of pumps. You must also remember that boots are designed to be sporty and almost always look gauche with dressy ensembles.

Good boots are ridiculously expensive these days. If you're lucky you might be able to find a decent pair for $150. More likely the ones you like best will be in the $250 to $400 range. This kind of money calls for extra caution in avoiding easily outdated, trendy styles—like the pseudo–cowboy boot that was the rage a few seasons back, or the flat wedge that was so popular last season. A fine, classically designed boot with a one- to two-

To look best, boots have to be proportionally in keeping with your total outfit (top left). Boots are generally too heavy to be worn with a silk dress (bottom left). No matter what the fashion magazines are showing, short boots worn with shirts or dresses are deadly for most women (above left). Try to avoid a space between the top of your boot and your hemline (above right).

inch straight heel defies time and will be good for a minimum of three years. The fit should be perfect, the silhouette slim and flattering to the leg. The leather and workmanship should, of course, be top quality. Boots are one place you really can't skimp. If you can't afford the best, you'd be better off without them. (Except, of course, the ones you need for foul weather.)

The height of the boot is important. There should never be a space between the top of the boot and the hem of your skirt. It tends to shorten the leg in a most inelegant way if the leg is cut by those two lines. Side zippers are usually a hallmark of cheap boots, unless they are extremely well sewn in. Regardless of what the magazines are showing, short boots should be worn with slacks only— unless you look like a ravishing model and are five feet nine. Pants tucked into tall boots cossack-style is another look that requires a model's figure, and even then it's risky. Even the most expensive and perfect boots tend to look cheap when worn in this fashion. If you want to look at all rich it's best to avoid this look.

Since boots are worn only in the fall and winter, calf and suede are equally good choices. Patent leather is irrevocably out of the question. Color should be a medium to dark neutral that blends well with your coats and jackets. Natural leather almost always looks good.

Comfort should not be forgotten. Boots, after all, are made for walking and should permit a naturally graceful stride. If they feel heavy or make you walk like a storm trooper, they are, need I say, the wrong boots for you.

Functional, sturdy rubber boots are fine for stormy, rainy days—not the ultimate in elegance, to be sure, but ever so much better than spotty, wet stockings.

Hosiery

IT IS BEST to keep hose in a neutral tone, one that will make your legs look slightly tanned. For fall and winter, though, you can go for a woollike textured stocking that is the same color as your outfit—black opaque hose with a black skirt and sweater, for example. It is not particularly elegant to introduce a new color or to pick up a minor color in your ensemble with your hose. Sheer patterned hose—with little dots or flowers—generally make the leg look a bit diseased and should be avoided.

Handbags

ASIDE FROM ill-looking shoes, nothing can downgrade a good outfit faster than a shoddy handbag. Handbags must be of top quality and will be expensive. Here again amortization comes into play—a bag is something that you use daily, and a good one will give you many years of elegant service. Far better to buy an excellent bag and wear it proudly year after year than to buy a mediocre one each year and not be tremendously satisfied. With our neutrally coordinated wardrobe plan, you'll actually need very few bags.

Bags and shoes don't have to match exactly but they should be of complementary tones. The size of your handbag should not be out of sync with your own size. A too large bag on a

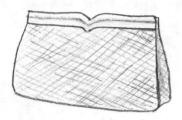

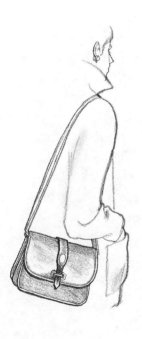

small woman looks as foolish as a minute purse on a large woman.

Overall you'll need a minimum of four bags:

1. A fairly good-sized, practical, casual bag—for your more sporty clothes and for travel. It should be of fine quality leather or excellent canvas with leather trim (no vinyl, please).

2. A slightly dressier, medium-sized bag—to wear with dresses and smart suits. The most practical choice would be, in most cases, a fine black calfskin (unless most of your wardrobe is in beige tones). Patent leather bags are not terribly elegant and suede is a bit fragile.

3. A small evening bag for more formal occasions. This bag can be of silk, satin, velvet, or superfine leather. If there is a gold clasp closing, it should be of the same refined and excellent quality as the bag. Uninspired clasps have been known to destroy the look of an otherwise lovely bag. Beaded bags only really look good in irridescent shades of solid colors like jet black, blue black, dark gray and coppery gold.

4. A natural straw handbag for summer. Straw is a fine match for summer linens and fine cottons.

Handbag designs go out of vogue much less frequently than clothing styles and can last ten years or more. No matter what the upcoming styles may be, it is always wise to discount exaggerated shapes and trendy trimmings and invest in classic shapes with conservative detailing.

Jewelry

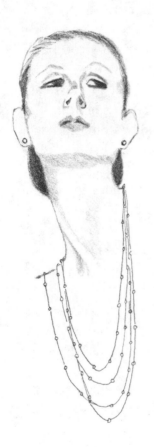

OF EVERYTHING in a woman's wardrobe, jewelry is the only purely decorative, nonfunctional element (with the exception of a watch). The choice of style is a very personal matter.

The first and foremost thing to remember here is *quantity*. No matter what the value of your jewelry, it should be worn in moderation. Adorning oneself with huge amounts of jewelry is simply in bad taste and is too reminiscent of a Christmas tree dripping with ornaments. Large pieces of jewelry should be worn alone and should be the real thing, not imitation. If you wear a necklace, bracelet, watch, earrings and ring at the same time, all should be very understated and of simple design. Too much jewelry smacks of imitation, even if it is the real McCoy.

While it would indeed be the height of luxury and grand fun to own a vast collection of spectacular jewels, you really don't *need* a lot of jewelry to look rich. You only need a few tasteful and versatile pieces to meet the various occasions in your life—which pretty much comes down to dressy or sporty. And remember, tasteful means never having to be flashy.

The most versatile and indispensable piece of jewelry you could own is still a good string of pearls. Pearls can add a dash of elegance to a simple wool blazer, a wonderful silk dress, and almost anything in between.

A pearl is formed by an oyster as it secretes a substance to cover an irritant—like a grain of sand—that happens to find its way into the shell. When this occurs naturally with no

help from man, the result is called a natural, or Oriental, pearl. The cultured pearl is formed when the irritant—usually a piece of shell—is placed in the oyster by man's hand. The simulated pearl leaves the oyster out of the picture entirely by dipping a plastic or glass nucleus again and again in a bath of fish scales and lacquer.

If you don't already own a string of pearls and are ready to consider making a purchase, you haved a choice between cultured pearls and the simulated variety. Since it has become unprofitable to reap Oriental pearls, they are now increasingly rare and prohibitively expensive. Needless to say, cultured pearls would be the first choice for all of us. If they are financially out of the ballpark, it is possible to find excellent imitation pearls that defy detection by the naked eye. They are, of course, much less expensive than the real thing.

Majorica pearls (a domestic brand name—not made in Spain) could be considered the Rolls-Royce of imitation pearls. They use the preferred glass (instead of plastic) nucleus, dip each pearl thirty-two times, and guarantee their product for ten years. While a fifteen-inch string of six-millimeter Majorica pearls would run in the vicinity of $70, the same size necklace of good quality cultured pearls would cost approximately $500 to $700. A thirty-inch strand of eight-millimeter simulated pearls from Majorica is about $135. The cultured variety would cost from $5,000 to $10,000, depending on the quality.

You can sometimes find real bargains in genuine pearls at auctions. Sotheby Parke

Bernet in New York, for instance, has noted that good single and double strands have been bought for $300 and $500, and the pearls are no less valuable than new ones. So it may just pay off to keep abreast of the important auction sales in your area.

Cultured pearls come in a variety of shapes, but a strand of perfectly round and matched jewels is still the most desirable. If you do buy expensive cultured pearls you should take care to inspect the strand carefully to see that the size and color are consistent throughout. Some pearls have a bluish white luster, others a yellow green, but the pinkish luster called *rosea* is the most desired. Pearls are judged on five criteria: size, shape, luster, color, and surface. The closer they come to being perfect in all these respects the more money they are worth.

To test a pearl for authenticity simply rub the pearl over the edge of your teeth. If it grates, it is real, and if it feels smooth, it is imitation. Also, a real pearl is cooler to the touch than a simulated one.

As with pearls, solid gold jewelry is a wise investment, but you can easily get by with good-quality gold-plated pieces until you acquire your fortune. It is a good idea to stick with the known brands that guarantee customer satisfaction.

If you do opt for gold-plated jewelry, make sure that the color is good and not brassy. Avoid jewelry that looks as if it would cost a mint if made from solid gold. Stick to simple designs that don't shout "costume jewelry." A wealthy acquaintance of mine wears so much gold that one naturally assumes at first glance that everything is costume even though each and every piece is solid gold. A few tasteful plated pieces are much less suspicious-looking than a slew of the same.

Imitation precious jewels are also acceptable for our purposes. It would be wise

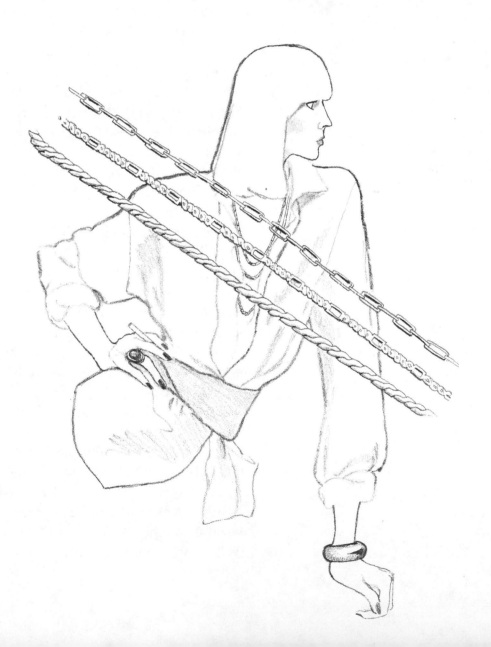

to acquaint yourself with the qualities of real jewels so you will be able to tell the best of the replicas when you see them. Zircons and other synthetic diamonds are so well made these days that it is very difficult to tell them apart from the real ones. Again, the most important thing is to keep the design simple to avoid suspicion. And make sure that the rest of your ensemble is chic enough to support your "diamonds."

Plastic costume jewelry can be amusing but never looks rich. Forget it. Tortoiseshell, ivory, jade, and even wood can look chic if they are superbly designed studies in simplicity. Gold astrological signs and small gold initials have no place in a chic wardrobe. Pass them on to your very young nieces.

The important thing to remember is that you don't need much. A gold wristwatch adds a solid, practical touch of elegance and can actually look richer than an armful of solid gold bracelets. Again, you could easily get by with a good, gold-plated classic, but you should consider an investment here if at all possible since a good watch will last forever. Diamond-studded watches *must* be 100 percent real, and in any case only look good on older women.

Rolex and Cartier watches have become definite status symbols; and I can't deny their fine quality—especially the Rolex. Frankly, I feel it is wise to steer clear of imitations here. You surely won't get the best of workmanship in the copies, and there are plenty of other tasteful watches around that will look rich as well as proclaim your individuality.

Eyeglasses

THE MOST important thing about eyeglasses is that they must be conservatively styled, whether they are round, slightly oval or rectangular. They must also compliment your face. Frames should be a neutral color and, of course, free of ornamentation. Rhinestones are definitely out.

Unless you are an aging movie queen or a young starlet with a hangover, dark sunglasses are best limited to outdoor wear on bright, sunny days.

Tortoiseshell is an excellent choice for daytime, and at its best actually looks quite fashionable.

Scarves and Shawls

SINCE scarves step out of the realm of major investments, they can be of any color or pattern—within reason. Patterns should not be loud but subtle. Scarves can be an elegant addition to your wardrobe if well chosen and worn with style. A silk (or silklike) square, for example, looks quite good tied and neatly tucked into a sweater with a high neckline in the fall or winter and can also work well tied around the outside of a collar and knotted in a bowlike fashion under the chin. Scarves worn

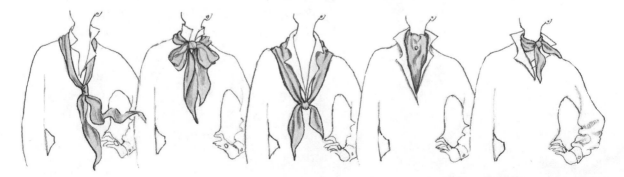

like cowboy bandanas do not look elegant. Long cashmere scarves are an indispensable accessory with coats and jackets.

The shawl is a time-honored, practical fashion staple that has recently experienced a popular revival. Shawls can look quite smart when they are well chosen and well draped. Since they can give favorite old clothes a new look, they certainly have a part in our plan. Cashmere, vicuña and very fine wool are ideal for winter and fall. Silk and silklike rayon would be good choices for warm summer evenings.

Shawls can be found in squares, rectangles, and triangles. Shape is really a matter of personal preference, but remember to keep proportion ever in mind. A large blanket shawl will overwhelm a small woman.

Illustrated here are some examples of chic ways to wear shawls.

Accoutrements

THE LITTLE accoutrements that you carry in your bag can bear the mark of wealth or the stamp of poverty. They should, therefore, be first-class. It should always be a pleasure, not an embarrassment, to pull out your date and address books, wallet, eyeglass case, cigarette lighter, compact or whatever various and sundry paraphernalia you carry in your purse.

Most of these articles, if they are quality, will last at least five years, are relatively inexpensive, and are definitely worth the money for the good feeling they give you and the first-rate image they present. Naturally, I don't advocate the insanity of buying a $2,000 cigarette case. (Although I must admit that if money were no object I would have put in my bid on a magnificent rose and yellow gold antique case that won my heart at a Parke Bernet auction. Unfortunately, money is an object.) Nor is it necessary to buy everything at once. Start with the most important article, say a beautiful pigskin or fine calfskin wallet, and make additions whenever possible. Wallets should be slim, not stuffed to the gills. There seems to be an inverse relationship between the size of a woman's wallet and the size of her income.

I predict the comeback of the all-too-long-forgotten fine lady's handkerchief, whose popularity has fallen by the wayside in favor of tissues. Handkerchiefs afford a very inexpensive touch of old-world elegance and are surely worth your consideration—at least as an accessory to their disposable counterparts. While they do have to be washed out, you can cut down on ironing by patting them on a smooth surface while they are still wet. When they dry they'll be ready for action again.

Luggage

LUGGAGE should also be a reflection of your high taste level, which, as we have already noted, always tends to suggest a high income level. Luggage should be tasteful, but it need not be costly. As a matter of fact, given the disrespect with which the airlines treat luggage, it would be a crime to send any kind of extremely expensive bag through their "torture chambers" (and I promised myself I wouldn't get vindictive). As well, there's the very real possibility of a bag getting lost altogether. There is, at present, a $750 maximum paid by airlines for lost or damaged luggage, unless you request additional insurance prior to the flight. It doesn't cost all that much, but it requires waiting in yet another line and filling out tedious and lengthy forms. Considering what you carry inside your bags, this is not a very solid reimbursement. No matter how you look at it, it just does not pay to overpay for luggage these days.

The days of steamer trunks, full wardrobes, matched sets of eight, and plentiful, happy porters are long gone. Only the memory lingers on. Today's travel requires light-weight, practical and hearty bags that are not too large or too heavy to carry when a porter can't be found—which is most of the time. (One should always travel with the assumption that all porters have been stricken with a deadly disease, that taxi drivers are holding their annual Hack Ball, and that airlines will deliver you to the farthest gate— if not the closest open field.)

There are some very handsome, sturdy bags on the market in the style of your choice. Our best bet would be a heavyweight, treated canvas with natural leather trimming, in a neutral dark shade (burgundy included). All-leather bags are beautiful, but the best are always too heavy and too expensive. Parachute rip-stop nylon is the lightest weight luggage fabric available, and in the dark shades bags made of it are fine for short trips. But clothes wrinkle more readily in one of these than in a more constructed bag, and some airlines insist that you sign a damage waiver if you ask to check it through. Cheap plastic bags—especially in bright or pastel colors—frankly look awful.

Bags no longer have to match, but styles should be similar in design details and the colors should blend well. So don't go to the expense of buying coordinated sets. Buy bags as you need them. Keep them simple, tailored, and a neutral color, and you won't go wrong.

I feel it would be unpardonable if I didn't give Louis Vuitton an honorable mention in the luggage category. The Louis Vuitton Company has been turning out exquisitely crafted luggage since 1854, and the name is still synonymous with superb quality and rare personalized service. While the LV handbags that you see on the arms of just about every woman on Rodeo Drive in Los Angeles have become a tired and tacky status symbol, fine pieces of LV luggage still spell rich— especially when they are being carried to one's private jet by one's "man."

As I said, it makes no sense and is hardly feasible to spend the required "millions" to purchase the best of the Louis Vuitton luggage, but if you have a chance, it is worth inspecting some of the more unusual and wonderful pieces to see what fine craftsmanship is all about and to have in mind what you might want to buy when your private jet comes in.

Belts

BELTS are a good and relatively inexpensive way to add new chic to classic, simple designs, and to rejuvenate the old timers in your wardrobe. The main rule of thumb here is that any belt that is prominently displayed must be of excellent quality, no matter what material it is made from. True to the overarching principle of Dressing Rich, you are much better off with fewer belts, all of quality, than mediocrity in quantity.

Many moderately priced shirtwaist dresses come with self-tie belts that tend to downgrade an entire look immediately. This is the perfect place for a winning belt substitute. It can turn a dress from chintzy to classy.

Generally speaking, belts should be in varying shades of the neutrals that form your foundation wardrobe. Tans and natural leather, for instance, blend with beiges

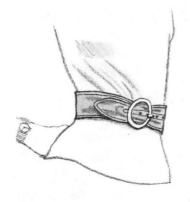

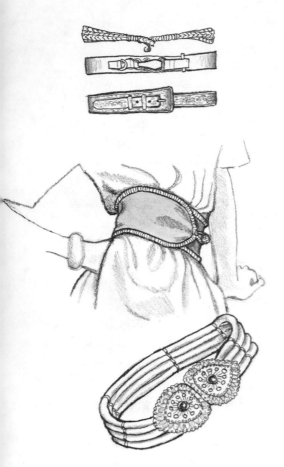

nicely. While belts in contrasting colors can be effective, they will also emphasize the waistline, and should be avoided if your waist and/or hips are ample.

The width of the belts you choose depends mainly on your figure. Tall, thin women can easily wear almost any width belt, but short women would do best to avoid wide belts. Generally, the smaller you are, the narrower the belt should be. Heavy women would also be doing themselves a service by steering clear of wide belts, if indeed they choose to wear belts at all.

If you are an ardent belt wearer, wonderful interchangeable belt buckles are worth considering. Since I wear relatively little jewelry, I often use a belt buckle to make a statement in its stead. Any of my growing collection of fine buckles looks perfect on any of my neutral-colored basic belts and gives an extra-special dimension to a simple mono-chromatic outfit. My turquoise and silver beauty looks especially good with black. Terrific buckles can be found at some specialty stores, antiques stores, and at auctions, and are a worthy investment. Most belts can be easily adapted for buckle changes by a good shoe repair shop.

Hats and Gloves

NOT THAT LONG AGO hats and gloves were fundamental elements of an elegant ensemble—especially the gloves. In her 1964 book, *Elegance*, Genevieve Dariaux pointed this out with unequivocal clarity: "Even women who never wear a hat should always wear gloves whenever they go out. Gloves

are one of the most unobtrusive accessories when you are wearing them, but their absence is glaringly apparent when you have left them at home. You should train your daughter to wear gloves as soon as she is old enough to walk. Nothing is more charming in the summer than to see a mother and daughter with bare arms and the same little short white cotton gloves."

Charming as they might have been in 1964, little white summer gloves are today nothing more than an amusing anachronism, for children and adults alike.

Winter gloves, on the other hand, while no longer as essential as they have been, are rather practical and can be as chic as they are comforting when the temperature begins to fall. A very good pair of silk-lined fine kidskin gloves is a wise and worthy investment. By now I'm sure it will come as no great surprise that I advocate a neutral color selection. Natural leather color or black would be the best choices, with brown as a third. This, of course, depends on your foundation colors. Natural tan would be smashing with the recommended oatmeal-flecked winter coat and would be a winning combination with almost any other brownish tweed and with gray flannel. Black would go nicely with black-flecked tweeds, navy, black and gray.

Gloves look best when the fit is perfect and the hand silhouette is slim. That's why I recommend silk lining. Wrists should be covered. Since you won't need more than two pairs of good gloves at most, they should be made of the finest kidskin. The fewer stitching details that are visible the better.

Casual, sporty, winter knockabout gloves needn't be as fine. Suede sheepskin ones are a good choice.

Hats can be an extremely practical accessory. They can help keep you warm in the winter and out of the sun in the summer, but as a fashion statement they are purely optional. Some women wear them elegantly and as naturally as if they had been born in them. On others hats look ill suited—as well as unflattering. The main cause of this diversity—aside from the complicated matter of personality and just plain confidence—is the matter of proportion and face shape. Flat berets, for example, look best on long, thin faces; wide brims are too overpowering for small women; and high crowns are ludicrous on large women (and frankly don't do that much for anybody).

If you do opt for hats, keep them simple—no extreme shapes, flowers, feathers, chin straps, or any other superfluous ornamentation, please. Color must ultimately be flattering to skin tone and harmonious with your outfit.

One of the worst offenders I've seen to date is a closely fitted hat of poor quality or of fake fur that so resembles hair that it is easily mistaken for a very ratty-looking coif (à la Phyllis Diller before she wisely cleaned up her act). Fur hats—most notably mink—are pretty much an anachronism these days. But if you have a penchant for them, they must be of top quality, and one must respect the obligation to increased elegance that is part of the deal when wearing mink.

4

THE POLISH: THOSE LEAST EXPENSIVE BUT CRUCIAL FACETS OF LOOKING RICH

Hair

EVEN THOUGH hair styles are as varied today as hem lengths, there are only a few, with variations, that look elegant. These styles all possess the same qualities: they are neat and simple, sensibly conservative, and flawlessly cut. The hair, of course, is healthy and clean. Richness in hair styles, like in clothing, is subdued and classic, never trendy or exaggerated. "Farrah Fawcett flips," "Dolly Parton poofs" or wild, frizzy do's (dubbed appropriately by Monsieur Marc of New York as *choucroute garni*, which means "sauerkraut with everything") never look elegant, to say the least. Following hair trends is sometimes more lethal than occasionally flirting with clothing trends, since you are often stuck with your decision for a considerable amount of time.

Like fashion designs, hair styles ultimately must be in perfect harmony with your proportions and features. But unlike apparel, you have little choice in the quality of the material. The texture of your hair is for the most part a given that has to be considered, as does face shape, neck size and head shape, in order to choose the most flattering hair shape.

Even with all these factors in mind, you will find among the following three general rich hairstyles a variation that would be ideal for you. It is advisable to consult with the best hairdresser available for guidance as well as for the consummate cut.

STYLE ONE: LONG HAIR

LONG HAIR looks most chic when worn away from the face and back or up. Once brushed back it can be pinned up into a classic chignon or French twist, tucked up into a modified Gibson (à la Katharine Hepburn), styled in a wonderful French braid, or tied at the nape of the neck in a "George Washington tie" or "status pull."

Remember, no matter how sexy your husband thinks your long hair is, it never looks elegant hanging carelessly down your back. Let your hair down in the bedroom only.

STYLE TWO: "LE LION"

ONE OF THE more classic cuts—sometimes called "the lion"—is the chin-length (or just below) blunt cut that is the same length all around. This is a most versatile haircut and can be worn straight, with a slight wave, flipped up on the ends, and even pulled back straight to accommodate a chignon or braid hairpiece. Dina Merrill, Gloria Vanderbilt, and Diana Vreeland, to name a few notable examples, all have their personal versions of this elegant cut.

STYLE THREE: THE SHORT LAYERED CUT

NANCY REAGAN has one of the most notable examples of a layered cut. The layering is very subtle and the cut creates a soft and flattering frame for the face. Hair can be layered in various ways to flatter most head shapes and necks. This cut provides a lift to the face and counters the downward lines that inevitably appear as we grow older, thus making it an ideal style for older women.

No matter what style you choose, hair should always look "alive"—not plastered down or sprayed to death. While a little backcombing at the roots is acceptable to add a little extra fullness, do not overtease your hair. Overteased is overcoiffed. Always check your hairdo from all angles—most expecially the profile. According to Monsieur Marc, whose clients include Mrs. Reagan among others, if the profile looks perfect, so will you.

Hair Coloring

IF HAIR is colored, the shade should be within the range of your natural hair color. Nothing is more gauche than hair that is overbleached, brassy, dyed a hard black or, heaven forbid, a carrot red. A good guideline for determining a new hair color is the color of your eyes. If your eyes are light, a light hair color will look natural; dark eyes are naturally complemented by darkish hair. And most any hair can be naturally colored in the winter for extra highlights and radiance that the sun usually provides in the summer.

Whether or not to cover gray is a personal decision. Some women look quite good with gray hair. I agree with Pablo, formerly of Elizabeth Arden, who says, "gray hair is chic after all. It is a lot better to be a genuine gray-haired lady than just another blonde, which is not exciting." Even so, there is no doubt that gray hair will make you look older. The time may come when you should let your hair go all gray, but if you are still young and gray hairs are only starting to be noticeable, then hair coloring in most cases is a fine idea. Remember too that skin tends to get lighter as you get older. If you do decide to cover gray with coloring, the coloring will look best if it is slightly lighter than your natural tone.

Makeup

MAKEUP TOO should be classic and understated. It should be used to enhance your natural beauty and to help create the illusion of flawless skin and wonderful bones. It should not be used to create an entirely new face. When cosmetics are applied well, they add a final polish and sophistication to your appearance. When they are applied with a heavy hand their purpose is defeated.

As with clothing it is wise to keep abreast of the current general direction of cosmetic fashion, but trendy makeup styles are as deadly to an elegant look as trendy apparel and haircuts. This immediately excludes dark lip liner, blue, green, and other fancifully colored eye shadow, obviously false eyelashes, and overly plucked eyebrows. Remember: the rich are not in the fashion vanguard. They don't break ice and introduce daring new styles. They are always safe and classic, in makeup as well as clothes and hair.

While I cannot guarantee what makeup look will appear richest in the year 2000, I can assure you that for the remainder of the eighties, and most probably the nineties, the tendency among elegant women is toward a natural, healthy, and polished look.

Don't mistake a light, easy, natural makeup look for a total absence of makeup. Wearing no makeup at all is fine for college girls or at the beach, but it never looks very chic to go totally without makeup in the city. Moderation, again, is the key word: neither too much nor too little, colors neither too dark nor too light.

The best way to apply makeup is as individual as your face. To use cosmetics most effectively is to know your face, and to under-stand all the nuances of its bone structure, skin coloring, and texture. If you are at all uncertain about how best to use makeup, it's a good idea to go in for a professional consultation. Most cosmetic companies regularly send their experts to department stores across the country to give demonstrations, and many beauty salons provide a cosmetic training service.

Skin care is especially important in our plan, where clean, healthy, well-tended skin is an indispensable element of the look. Monthly facials and commercial skin care products can be expensive, but if you can't spare the money, you should put aside some time. Excellent natural treatments can be made at home at a minimal cost, and are actually recommended over their commercial counterparts.

I've compiled this short list of home skin care recipes from a selection of the many "natural beauty" books that are currently available in good health food shops or in regular bookstores. This is just a small sample to serve as inspiration and to give you an idea of the high-quality and very inexpensive skin care "products" that are as close as your kitchen cupboard.

OATMEAL: when mixed with honey, milk, or water, makes a good cleansing and refining mask.

YOGURT: a good cleanser for oily skin. Makes a good beauty mask when one teaspoon of plain is mixed with half an egg yolk, one-half teaspoon honey, and a dash of cornstarch. Leave mask on for fifteen minutes and then remove with warm water.

CIDER VINEGAR: when mixed with equal parts of water, cleans and tones the skin.

LEMON JUICE: helps clear pimples and eruptions when applied directly with a cotton swab.

POTATOES: grated raw and applied to eye area, help eliminate puffiness and bags.

CUCUMBER JUICE: makes a good skin toner. The whole mashed cucumber can be used as a refreshing toning mask. Placing slices of cucumber over the eyes for fifteen minutes helps soothe and refresh tired eyes.

As I said, these are just a few examples of nature's own products that can cleanse and tone your skin as well as the costly commercial counterparts. When you consider how great an influence a clean, healthy, glowing complexion has on your overall appearance, I think you will agree with me that home remedies like these are a real bargain and certainly deserve consideration. Again, you can use time, a little effort, and know-how to save money.

Although lipsticks, powders, mascaras, et al. are nearly impossible to reproduce at home, it is possible to reduce makeup expenditures by not buying only the status brands. As unchic as it may sound, you can often find quite satisfactory cosmetics in five-and-ten-cent stores. The packaging may not be dazzling and brilliant advertising campaigns may not be launched for them each season, but the products themselves are often quite fine.

For example, I had no luck in finding a red lipstick that didn't "bleed," smear, or quickly wear off until I discovered Hazel Bishop non-smear lipstick in the five-and-ten for eighty-nine cents a tube. It's a real bargain and comes in four great red shades. I should mention that the tip came from a friend of mine who is an executive at one of the well-known and prestigious cosmetic companies. Mascaras and face powders are other good dime-store buys.

The Physical Attributes

THE DUCHESS OF WINDSOR hit the nail on the head when she said, "You can never be too thin or too rich." While emaciation is taking a good thing too far—and is hardly the richest look in town—a healthy, fit, slim body is a mark of money. It's been a long time since aristocracy subscribed to the theory that skinny means poor and undernourished and that plumpness is a symbol of well-being. The tables have completely turned. Today the rich are especially health conscious. They eat well, but sparsely, and keep fit in the most exclusive spas. They have a general disdain for the overweight and never indulge themselves—at least not in anything as mundane or fattening as food.

Of course there are exceptions to the "thin is rich" rule, but there's no doubt that you'll have a better overall chance of pulling off the look if you keep your weight down. Look at it this way: not only will your clothes look better, but all the money you save on food can go right into your wardrobe.

It's been said that long, thin, graceful bones and delicate, finely chiseled features are part and parcel of a rich look. Certainly these qualities would be an unquestionable asset in a rich look—or any look for that matter—but they are not a prerequisite nor a guarantee of elegance. Even the patrician air of such long-stemmed, fine American beauties as Dina Merrill, Candice Bergen and Grace Kelly (in her film days) would be destroyed if they slouched about with greasy hair and chewed gum in a bovine manner.

If your bone structure is not as perfect as you'd have it, forget about it. Unlike weight, bones are not easily altered. There's no sense in fretting over what you don't have. Make the best of what you've got and be thankful it's in a healthy state.

Basic bone structure aside, there are a variety of features that can be modified—nipped, tucked, added, and subtracted—through excellent (if rather costly) plastic surgery: overly prominent noses, receding chins, sagging jowls, and all wrinkles and lines, just to name a few. It's no secret that cosmetic surgery is as commonplace among the rich as betting on favored thoroughbreds, and bears no more stigma. If you're terribly self-conscious about a feature that can be improved through good cosmetic surgery, and you can afford it, I frankly see no reason not to give it some serious thought.

Plastic surgery, however, should not be taken too lightly. If it is not done well it can be disastrous. Need I say that this is no place to look for the best bargain. Word of mouth from satisfied customers is probably the best way to select a surgeon. But it's still a good idea to interview at least three doctors before you decide on one. Most have pictorial records of past operations in which you can

see a patient before and after. This is usually
a good indicator of a doctor's work. If a
surgeon's attitude is too cavalier or flip or if
he doesn't require medical photographs
beforehand for facial surgery, he shouldn't
even be considered.

Another good check is to see if the surgeon
is certified by the American Board of Plastic
Surgeons. (Certified surgeons are listed in
the *Directory of Medical Specialists* in the
Marquis Who's Who series.) Although this is
not an absolute guarantee of satisfaction—
nothing is—it is heartening to know that
doctors that qualify for certification have at
least three years of approved training in
general surgery, two years of credited resi-
dency in plastic surgery, and have passed
both written and oral examinations.

In most cases teeth have definite priority
over cosmetic surgery in my mind. Bad teeth
are a sure sign of past poverty: that your
parents didn't have adequate funds for proper
orthodontic care for you when you were
young. Again, make sure you make a wise
choice when it comes to the dentist who will
correct your dental flaws. Badly capped teeth
are often worse than untreated bad ones.

Thinking Rich: The Right Attitude

TRUE ELEGANCE, STYLE, and an affluent air are the result not only of fashion, but of bearing and attitude. Your carriage, speech and voice quality, gestures, and personal aura play a very vital role in your overall presentation. While fashion changes from year to year, the words that are used to describe women of elegance have always remained constant: graceful, good-humored, kind, vital, determined, energetic, intelligent and dedicated. Unlike a luxurious mink coat or a diamond necklace, these essential qualities, and other winning ones, are free of charge and available to any woman who cares enough to put theory into practice.

The first step in developing an effective patrician manner and affluent attitude is thinking and feeling rich. You will never look like a million if you feel deprived, bitter, and generally unhappy about your luck in life. Crying about what you don't have will not do you one bit of good or, if it could, that good will only put a burdensome chip on your shoulder.

Be optimistic and delighted with what you do have—your spiritual, mental and physical health, and your uniqueness—and then put them all to work for you, to improve and grow. In other words, before you can look rich you have to love and believe in yourself. It is this self-love, first and foremost, that will give you the self-confidence to go out in the world and look as if you own it.

Women who don't believe in themselves will always give the impression that they are trying too hard, which in effect they are:

trying not only to prove their worth to others, but to themselves as well. Trying too hard won't get you any further than not trying at all. Quiet, confident vitality is the key phrase for the key attitude.

Since we have to start somewhere, I have noted here some tried-and-true, reliable attitude guidelines to set you off in the right direction.

• Good humor and optimism are two notable characteristics of prosperity. Even in the face of extreme adversity, never panic. Everything will work out. It always does.

• You can never go wrong with a winning smile. Since the rich have a lot to be happy about, they are always smiling. It's only our discontented and frustrated brethren who constantly sport a scowl. Even if you're not feeling in a particularly cheery mood, you'll find that smiling can really make you feel better—and the people around you will feel better, too.

• Deal with people in a direct and simple manner. There's no need either to apologize sheepishly for a reasonable request or to shout rude commands like a sixteenth-century monarch. Everyone—delivery boys and aristocracy alike—should be dealt with courteously.

• The art of understatement linked with a slight aura of mystery is a combination nonpareil. The rich don't have to prove anything. Hold back a little. Let them come to you and don't show all your cards at once.

• Voice quality is quiet and demure—never loud and vulgar. The lower the timbre the better. Articulation and clear enunciation are essential. Mumbles are strictly lower class. Extreme regional accents are a giveaway as well since among the rich they are diligently polished away by the best boarding schools and undone by much European travel. A magnetic, engaging voice can lend unparalleled charm, mystery, and charisma, and is definitely worth cultivating.

• A straight, but relaxed, posture is another essential. Sagging shoulders, rounded backs, and dropping chins create a downtrodden and underprivileged image—and they ruin the drape of good clothes as well.

• Intelligence is a respected virtue. It doesn't take a genius IQ, or even a college education for that matter, to be well read and knowledgeable about current events and world politics. Make a point of reading a good newspaper daily. A well-founded opinion—whether it is popular or not—is better than no opinion at all.

Conclusion

WITH *Dressing Rich* you can see that the "look of class" is available to everyone who cares, regardless of social standing or income. Money, it turns out, is neither a prerequisite nor a guarantee of elegance. There are as many wealthy bad dressers as there are poor ones. In the final analysis, there is a big difference between looking elegantly rich and simply looking as if you have money.

There is no denying that it is an easier feat to build a classicly chic wardrobe when you are backed by unlimited funds. I'd certainly be the last one to renounce the joys of unconditional purchasing power. But since that is pure wishful thinking for most of us, let's look at it this way: there is much more challenge and ultimate satisfaction in turning out a top-drawer wardrobe on a relatively limited budget. And it can be fun and creative. So don't be discouraged for lack of major financing. When you're armed with awareness and the Dressing Rich technique, the true rich look is yours for the taking.

Dressing Rich is not just dressing for others. Presenting yourself in the best possible manner makes you feel good about yourself. When you are good to yourself, treat yourself well and dress well, you feel—and look—like a million.

Dressing well is also symbolic of a high-quality life. We only go through once. We might as well do it in the most gracious manner and enjoy the finest things in life. Dressing Rich and living well— even on a budget—just may still be the best revenge.